D1058768

IT'S
YOUR
LOSS

DK LONDON
Publishing Director Katie Cowan
Art Director Maxine Pedliham
Senior Acquisitions Editor Stephanie Milner
Managing Art Editor Bess Daly
Copy Editor Amy Christian
Proofreader Katie Hewett
Indexer Lisa Footitt
Jacket Designer Holly Ovenden
Designer Jordan Lambley
Photographer Alexandra Cameron
Production Editor David Almond
Production Controller Kariss Ainsworth

First published in Great Britain in 2021 by
Dorling Kindersley Limited
DK, One Embassy Gardens, 8 Viaduct Gardens,
London, SW11 7BW

The authorised representative in the EEA is
Dorling Kindersley Verlag GmbH. Arnulfstr. 124,
80636 Munich, Germany

Copyright © 2021 Dorling Kindersley Limited
A Penguin Random House Company
10 9 8 7 6 5 4 3 2 1
001–324529–Sep/2021

All rights reserved. No part of this publication
may be reproduced, stored in or introduced into
a retrieval system or transmitted, in any form or by
any means (electronic, mechanical, photocopying,
recording or otherwise), without the prior written
permission of the copyright owner.

A CIP catalogue record for this book is available
from the British Library.
ISBN: 978-0-24151-040-7

Printed and bound in the United Kingdom

For the curious
www.dk.com

This book was made with Forest Stewardship Council ™ certified
paper – one small step in DK's commitment to a sustainable future.
For more information go to www.dk.com/our-green-pledge

This book is a work of
non-fiction based on the life,
experiences and recollections
of Robyn Donaldson and Emma
Hopkinson. In some cases,
names of people and places
have been changed solely to
protect the privacy of others.

Text copyright © 2021
Robyn Donaldson and
Emma Hopkinson

Robyn Donaldson and Emma
Hopkinson have asserted their
right to be identified as authors
of this work.

Text on pages 64–65,
reprinted by permission of
Catherine Cho, 2021; 96–97,
reprinted by permission of
Alicia Stubbersfield, 2021;
128–129, reprinted by
permission of Richard Coles,
2021; 158–159, From A Blood
Condition by Kayo Chingonyi
published by Chatto &
Windus. Copyright © Kayo
Chingonyi, 2021. Reprinted by
permission of The Random
House Group Limited; 190–
191 reprinted by permission of
Natalie Lee/Style Me Sunday,
2021; 222–223, Running Upon
the Wires by Kae Tempest
published by Pan Macmillan
and Bloomsbury US. Copyright
© Kae Tempest, 2021.
Reprinted by permission of Kae
Tempest; 252–253, reprinted
by permission of Sophie
Williams, 2021; 278–279,
reprinted by permission of
Adam Buxton, 2021.

Jacket photography copyright
© 2021 Alexandra Cameron

IT'S YOUR LOSS

living with grief is hard,
we <u>hope</u> this book will help

**ROBYN DONALDSON
& EMMA HOPKINSON**

*To my Mama, Berenice, who
always wanted a book of her own
– Emma*

*And to my Nana, Barbara, who always
made us shine our brightest
– Robyn*

CONTENTS

WELCOME TO LOSS TOWN

So life took an undesirable turn and you ended up in a strange place? Let us show you around...

Emma: I remember having the feeling of: this is somebody else who gets it. This is a lifeline.

Robyn: Yes! It was like you were an old hand. I could ask you things and you seemed so relaxed with it, though of course I now know that was you repressing things in a big way.

Emma: I was always looking for somebody to hold my hand through it – I'd have lots of drunk conversations with anybody who was experiencing something similar. But nobody would have me. And then there you were, and we did a little rescue on each other.

Robyn: We really did. It became manageable. If this woman, who I respected and who had it all figured out, was doing this too then I could handle it.

Emma: I think even though it was a fledgling friendship at that time, there was just a steel connection because we had this big sadness in common. And although there were periods where we saw each other less, that was always there.

Nobody likes Loss Town. True story. It's not a place we intend to go, and yet it's a place that all of us do. Unfortunately, at some point or another, if you live a life, you're going to experience some kind of loss, and very often, it sucks. Like a whirling vortex, it whips you away, and manages to make you feel terribly alone just when you need the most support. It spins you out of your routine and lived experiences, and dumps you into an emotional hinterland where you may or may not find yourself eating chocolate spread out of the jar, for years on end. Also, like a whirling vortex, it does not come with an instruction manual. Until now.

OK, it's not quite an instruction manual, but this book *will* talk about what it's like to go through a loss. Any loss, whether it's the death of a loved one, the end of a career, a marriage, an estrangement – anything. And it's here to help, no matter what kind of loss-ee you are. It's designed to help you get your head around what to expect, navigate some of the emotions, and ultimately come out the other side knowing yourself a little bit better. We work on the idea that, whoever or whatever you lose, the feelings and responses attached to the situation are broadly the same, because they come from you. The experience of losing a career, for example, can mirror the feelings you have when you lose a loved one. In general, the world's pretty lenient when you're bereaved, but people can be less understanding when you're still in your pyjamas six months after a divorce. So, we've taken a romp through our own experiences, and aim to help you look at yours, understanding the many and varied ways that they fit into and inform your life. Because they do inform your life, for better or worse, and we're here to help it be for the better as much as possible. Think of this book like one of the topographically unsound, abstract (but jolly) maps you get for theme parks. There'll be some oversized illustrations of the main characters and points of interest, the location of the toilets and the food, and the rest you'll fill in yourself as you wander around. We'll be the tour guides waving a giant umbrella.

The two of us are total opposites. In the way we think, speak, dress, socialize, dance, live and grieve. So, when we both lost our Mum-figures to cancer in our mid-twenties, we couldn't have dealt with it in more different ways. And after much thinking and wondering, we believe that a lot of that was down to the fact that we're each a fairly extreme version of introvert and extrovert. In case you're hoping for an oversimplified definition of what that means: an introvert is somebody who deals with things on the inside, and an extrovert is somebody who deals with things on the outside. The introvert does a lot of thinking by themselves; the extrovert does a lot of talking with other people. In the middle of our two ways of Doing Life sits everything else – the introverts with extrovert tendencies, the extroverts with introvert tendencies, the ones who are one some days and another the next. We hope that you'll see some of what we're talking about and go, "Yes! Me too!"

You might be asking yourself, but why should I listen to this pair of women with a pretty conventional experience of loss? Well, because of just that – we get it in a reassuringly basic and universal way. As you sit there in a heap we're nodding, because we get it. As you ponder whether it's possible for the human heart just to grind to a halt with sadness, we get it. As you plot a murder rampage because all the other thoughtless bastards seem to be carrying on with their lives like civilization isn't Fundamentally Over like it is for you, **we get it**. Why do we get it? Because, friends, we've been on this journey before. Losing our best women was the hardest time of our young lives, but through it we learned so much about ourselves; about relationships and about the world. We both often say that we'd have been a bit adrift had we not had each other to check in with now and again and say, "Well this is shit, isn't it?" – and that's what we want this book to be. A little life raft in the choppy waters of the Great Sea of Loss. So we've packed our emotional knapsack, hoisted the Kleenex sails and recruited First Mate Dr Sheetal Dandgey, our resident psychotherapist, to offer some bona fide mental health insight into our various coping mechanisms. Because we're very much not medical professionals, we're just two people who went through some stuff and want to help other people going through something similar. And we've found that talking about it with people has really helped. In fact, we'd both say, uncomfortably, that some of the best things we have in life wouldn't be there if we hadn't first gone through loss. Loss sucks, yes, but there are ways to help yourself respond to it differently, ways to find it less terrifying, and ways to shift your mind away from the trauma. Once you do that, you're not only able to remember the good bits about the person or thing you lost, you can perhaps start living life in a whole new way. Then because we know that there are as many ways to do loss as there are stars in the sky, we'll hear from others along the way, too, with stories, snippets and poetry from people who've trodden these boards before.

This book is about the things we've learned through loss, repackaged for you. We can dig into what happened, hold the bad bits at arm's length to look at them, before dusting off the better bits to reassure you that you probably will come out the other end in some ways improved. With more moving parts and lots of Sellotape holding you together, but there and still ticking over. And we'll serve those bits up to you, like a mama bird puking her soupy info goodness straight into your sad little mouth. Deeelicious.

Because of all of the above we're going to try to be the people we desperately needed when we were stuck in Loss Town. You'll hear our stories next, so you know where we're coming from, and we'll talk about the general logistics of loss in *Lossgistics*. Then we'll unpack the suitcase carrying all the emotional baggage in *The Unmistakable Whiff of Guilt, Anger, Anxiety and the Rest,* and if you've been wondering why everything else feels so terrible since your loss, that chapter might be a help. We'll talk support networks in *Loss Club*, finding your cultural nesting spot in *The Wide World* and self-care in *Treat Yo'self.* Then we'll find different ways to memorialize the thing you lost in *Misty Watercolour Memories* before we rediscover the nearly-new you in *You 2.0.* And before one final farewell in the *Mic Drop* outro, we'll look at ways to help friends in need, in *I Got You, Dave* – a must-read if you're caring for anybody, ever (we think). This isn't the seven steps. It's more "Pick Your Own Adventure". We'll be there to hold your hand as you tread your own mind-bogglingly individual path, shouting supportive and hopefully insightful things along the way.

This book is for *you.* If you've gone through loss, if you know somebody going through a loss, or if you hope to understand how it feels. This book is for you if you're trying to find the normal in the most abnormal but inevitable human experience. It's for you if you're an introvert, for you if you're an extrovert, and for you if you sit somewhere in the middle. It's for you if you just want to hear one little thing that feels familiar when the world is anything but. It's for you if you want to know you're not alone. It's for you if you've felt all the feelings we talk about and want to look back on it, now you're at a safe distance, and see if you can pick out the useful bits. It's a book for anyone who feels any kind of loss acutely, so really it's for all of us. We expect it will be in every hotel room drawer soon, like a non-denominational Gideons Bible.

So what next? Well read it, probably. And while you're reading it, take a breath, take time. To reflect. To look at your situation. We want you to use it in a book club for your friends and to send photos to pals who might dig it and feel seen. To gift it. To keep it. To put your coffee on it when your nose isn't buried in it. To get out a highlighter. To make notes. Or just read in one big go. To use it however *you* find useful. Because this book, that's in one way so personal and born directly out of our own loss, is yours, whoever you are. We could think of no greater way to acknowledge how incredible the people that we're without were, than to use them as a beacon. A distant, reassuring flame on the side of a mountain when you feel like it's all fog and exhaustion and frostbite and there's not another soul around. This book is about you, about your emotional expedition, the things you might encounter and how you can best navigate this unknowable world in a way that works uniquely for your situation. When all's said and done, the clue is in the title: it's *your* loss, we're just here to provide a little companionship. So seatbelts on, we're in for quite a ride.

It's
for
you

if you just want to
hear one little thing
that feels familiar
when the world is
anything but.

EMMA'S STORY
A sad tale from one very anxious introvert

My Mum died from breast cancer when she was 51. That's young, right? It went undetected for about 18 months so by the time they found it, it had spread to her bones, and then a few years later, she died. I was 26, which is also young. Young to lose a Mum, young to go through a big loss, and young to handle all the gumpf that came with it.

She was a smart, funny woman, was Berenice (pronounced Berreh-neece, if you please), who made a mean lemon meringue pie and gave the best hugs this side of heaven, and I loved her hugely, painfully, even when she was alive. We shared almost the exact same sensibilities, so talking to her always felt like slipping into a warm bath where everything was comfortable and easy – a nurturing break from the socially anxious mind I've carried around with me since I was an egg. And though she lived very far away from me, all I needed to do was pick up the phone for a chat and we'd be together again, love batteries charged, ready to get on with the rest of life. I could deal with the world because in her I always had a safe space to retreat back to where I felt seen and understood. So when she died, I lost my Mum, yes, but I also lost that safe space – the place I felt I belonged in the world.

My parents divorced when I was tiny, and after a brief stint with my Mum, I went to live with my Dad, step-mum and older step-sister, seeing my Ma at weekends, when we'd do arts and crafts and dig in the garden and swim and eat spaghetti and overdose on sweets. I think it's often the way with kids of divorce, that the distant parent gets to live on a pedestal, and that's where I kept my Mum, right up until she popped off. Because I couldn't have her with me, I idolized her and made her everything. I even look exactly like her –

18

can you will yourself to do that? If you can, I probably did. Like lots of kids with divorced parents, that first loss set the stage for how I would deal with other losses in life. Which is to say I'd worry about them on the inside and pretend everything was OK on the outside. I think it's quite common for children in this situation to feel like they have to make everything OK for everybody else, so they develop behaviours to support that. In my case, I grew myself a suit of emotional armour that looked shiny and bright, and held a quivering fear jelly in its steely innards. I built my little suit of armour and hid in it, then I carried it all the way from childhood to adulthood. If I'm honest, I'm still wearing it, to some degree. If any of this rings true for you, you'll know – it makes you an expert at compartmentalizing – putting stuff that threatens the integrity of the suit into little lockboxes so we don't have to deal with them. And after my Mum had been sick for five years, you'd better believe I was wearing the suit of armour when she died. Heck, I'd built it an outhouse with its own pool and butler, and a granny annexe off the west wing. I gave a eulogy at the funeral, went back to work straight away, and ploughed all of my energies into a destructive relationship – anything to not to look at what had happened.

I was in my second year of university when I found out she was sick. While I was studying in the South of England, my Mum was living up in Scotland on a very tiny, very remote island where the bulk of the population is bracken and cows. After suffering with back pain she'd finally been taken into hospital for a scan, which showed up the cancer. And although they could treat it, there was no recovery in the offing – it would eventually kill her. In the end, we got about five years together. She got to see me graduate from university and move to London; she got to see me start my career writing about fashion in the big city, and I think she was the proudest person because of it. But in those five years her marriage broke down. She was kicked out of her home and had to live by herself for a while, then finally reconciled with her husband before she died. They were hard years, and not just because of the trudging inevitability of it all, but because the covers were pulled back on all the comfortable lies we'd been telling ourselves. There was heartache and horror at every turn and it broke my little heart to the point that when she did die, I couldn't really think about any of what had happened, choosing instead to soldier on and pretend everything was OK.

But of course, then, because loss is never straightforward, there were all the traumas and smaller losses that were folded into the big one, in the worst cake batter of all time. Being in the room, by myself, when she died. Hearing her rattly breathing stop and not really understanding what was happening. The estrangement from my step-dad and witnessing the breakdown of what I'd believed until then was a perfect marriage. My Grandma scattering my Mum's ashes and nobody having the guts to tell me it had happened. A brief sexual assault.[1] And – before she died – living through the whole last few weeks of her life completely on my own in a small holiday cottage on a tiny Scottish island, in which the only signal was on the other side of the house, where I'd place my phone on its loudest ring every night, waking up constantly to check it in case I missed her going. Spoiler: I didn't. She held on for me to be there and I got to tell her how much I loved her before she went – in your face, universe. We'll speak more on this stuff through the book, but my point is that that loss, which looks on the surface like the simple passing of a beloved Mum, actually carried with it, and caused, so many other bits

---

1 In case you're worried, this is the last time in the book it'll be mentioned.

and pieces too. And because of those things, and because of how I'm built, that loss, for me, brought raging anxiety to the surface that turned into a full-blown disorder.

I was always an anxious person, sure, but in the shadow of that Mum-loss it really took on new proportions. I was exhausted, constantly, but also full-body fizzing. You know that stomach-churning, heart-racing nervousness you get when you're waiting to go into a job interview? I lived with that, constantly, for years. I couldn't sleep, couldn't eat – I'd make food I loved and just stare at it. I started walking the 3 miles to work because standing still on the tube was too much to handle. And the lack of sleep only made it harder – my poor old brain getting even less coherent and less able to deal with what was going on. But nobody knew about it. I felt like I needed to broadcast a reassuring "I'M OK" message to the world, and I started to believe that message myself. That was just how life was, I thought. Standard. It'll just always be shit from here on in. So I made no moves to combat it – it didn't even occur to me that I deserved better. I just ploughed on, ignoring my physical and emotional needs, keeping it all in the lockbox, until eventually I struggled to have emotions even by myself.

I've learned a lot since then, about loss, about myself, about why I went through it in the way that I did, and this book is my response. My way of saying to anybody struggling out there, that you're not doing it wrong. That there's no correct response to loss, and that you, ultimately, have got this. Being somebody who lives their emotional life on the inside presents its own set of challenges through loss, but I hope that by putting some of my inside on the outside, some people like me will feel a sense of comfort. That's what this is – one giant, "I See You" from this gal to you.

THERE'S NO CORRECT RESPONSE TO LOSS,
THERE'S NO CORRECT RESPONSE TO LOSS,
THERE'S NO CORRECT RESPONSE TO LOSS,
THERE'S NO CORRECT RESPONSE TO LOSS,
THERE'S NO CORRECT RESPONSE TO LOSS,
THERE'S NO CORRECT RESPONSE TO LOSS,
THERE'S NO CORRECT RESPONSE TO LOSS,
THERE'S NO CORRECT RESPONSE TO LOSS,
THERE'S NO CORRECT RESPONSE TO LOSS,
THERE'S NO CORRECT RESPONSE TO LOSS,
THERE'S NO CORRECT RESPONSE TO LOSS,
THERE'S NO CORRECT RESPONSE TO LOSS,
THERE'S NO CORRECT RESPONSE TO LOSS,
THERE'S NO CORRECT RESPONSE TO LOSS,
THERE'S NO CORRECT RESPONSE TO LOSS,
THERE'S NO CORRECT RESPONSE TO LOSS,
THERE'S NO CORRECT RESPONSE TO LOSS,
THERE'S NO CORRECT RESPONSE TO LOSS,
THERE'S NO CORRECT RESPONSE TO LOSS,
THERE'S NO CORRECT RESPONSE TO LOSS,
THERE'S NO CORRECT RESPONSE TO LOSS,
THERE'S NO CORRECT RESPONSE TO LOSS,
THERE'S NO CORRECT RESPONSE TO LOSS,
THERE'S NO CORRECT RESPONSE TO LOSS,
THERE'S NO CORRECT RESPONSE TO LOSS,
THERE'S NO CORRECT RESPONSE TO LOSS,
THERE'S NO CORRECT RESPONSE TO LOSS,
THERE'S NO CORRECT RESPONSE TO LOSS,
THERE'S NO CORRECT RESPONSE TO LOSS,
THERE'S NO CORRECT RESPONSE TO LOSS,

AND ULTIMATELY
AND ULTIMATELY
AND ULTIMATELY
AND ULTIMATELY
AND ULTIMATELY
AND ULTIMATELY
AND ULTIMATELY
AND ULTIMATELY
AND ULTIMATELY
AND ULTIMATELY
AND ULTIMATELY
AND ULTIMATELY
AND ULTIMATELY
AND ULTIMATELY
AND ULTIMATELY
AND ULTIMATELY
AND ULTIMATELY
AND ULTIMATELY
AND ULTIMATELY
AND ULTIMATELY
AND ULTIMATELY
AND ULTIMATELY
AND ULTIMATELY
AND ULTIMATELY
AND ULTIMATELY
AND ULTIMATELY
AND ULTIMATELY
AND ULTIMATELY
AND ULTIMATELY YOU HAVE GOT THIS.

ROBYN'S STORY

A sad tale from an also-anxious extrovert

My story is complicated and hinges on the fact that I have never had a healthy relationship with my biological mother. Even from being very little. It was hugely volatile and at times abusive, emotionally and physically. I feel very detached from that little girl and I can talk about that abuse because it doesn't feel Too Much. There weren't broken bones or hospital trips or physical scars. But I also feel like it's branded on every inch of me, invisibly. It's left me with very hollow, terribly fragile bones like a little thrush. It would only take a firm grip to squash me. And I've gravitated to that grip so often, like so many children of abuse. The familiarity and comfort of it. It's tight and grounding and, ultimately killing you. Thankfully, I found my nice husband who's not an abuser and he sits me on his palm and I flit about and it's all very nice, and I'm glad to have chosen the thing I needed not the thing I was pulled towards. This makes my husband sound like Dick Van Dyke in *Mary Poppins*, and he sort of is.

When I was nine, my Dad nearly killed himself in a motorbike accident and my Mum up and left. As a result, I hadn't got to mourn the fact she *was there* and it seemed like she hated me, but the fact she wasn't. Even knowing how wrong my parent's relationship was and that the shouting and scuffles and angst would go away, the loss of proximity to a parent can be completely heart-breaking and unfathomable for a child. Even if that parent is objectively shit. In a certain, anxious little mind it can equal, "You were not good enough for me to stay." It's very hard. But thankfully I had Andy, my brilliant Dad who, while being totally fucked up because of his own childhood and a raging alcoholic who kept crashing into things at various – sometimes deadly – speeds, was someone who made me feel so loved, so looked after and that I was good enough. My Dad is amazing. When he couldn't love himself, he found an endless supply of effusive love for my brother and me. Where did that even come from? He's miraculous. I know not everyone gets an Andy, though I wish they did.

Because it seemed from day one that my Mum had little interest in her baby and my Dad was an absolute catastrophe, my Nana, Barbara, who was 36[2] at the time, instinctively stepped in. Which I can see now probably compounded the problems my Mum had feeling close to me and, ironically, to her own mum. My Nan and I openly adored each other, while I think my Mum felt hard done by on all counts. I got all the delightful grandparent do-over with none of the mistakes my Mum had experienced and my Nan got a child without a lot of angry baggage. Barbara and I had a very special bond. It was both unspoken and explicitly spoken about. The last time we saw one another, when she knew she was going to die and I couldn't even approach considering it, my Nan told me how special what we had was. I told her to stop being so cheesy and then we cried and hugged and I thought she must be on some new drugs or something because she was being really, really nice. She was the person I'd call in uni to yell how grateful I was over the nightclub soundtrack and who I'd email on holiday to tell how big a fish I'd caught. She'd say to friends "Make sure you look after her." She was just a mum. It feels so extraordinary to have had that relationship. Which is mad as I know for most people it's the

---

2 My actual current age.

bedrock. I'm so sad I didn't see it for what it was sooner and let go of that ache for a "conventional relationship" with my Mum – I think we'd both have had a smoother ride for it. I would certainly have been less cruel. Because as much as you might be reading this and thinking "Fucking hell, Robyn had a terrible time, that's appalling," I, in turn, learned to be appalling. I learned the language of abuse. I can be violently cruel. I can make someone feel like they're nothing at all. And I have thrown those emotional WMDs at all sorts of people but primarily my mother. Even when she didn't really deserve it but because I was so angry at her for everything that had come before and her inability to acknowledge it. I'm trying to be less angry and the older I get, the more just terribly sad I feel for my Mum and the constant injustices she sees. But I am not blameless. I have caused her pain. It's important that I acknowledge that.

I don't think I ever deployed the full arsenal of my emotional weaponry on my Nan though. I loved her and she plugged a parent gap until I was 24 and in retrospect it was all just pretty marvellous. Then she called one day and was like "I'm having a hysterectomy, nothing out of the ordinary, just your standard hysterectomy, you know?" and I thought, "Sure, people have them all the time." Except they really don't. I have no idea what the thinking around that messaging was. I guess she hoped that every last bit of cancer would come out with her womb and she'd spare us all the stress of even mentioning it. But, because we're living in a collective shitcom, she had a massive bleed after surgery, her children were called, she saw them and freaked out she was dead and then, whacked out on morphine, proceeded to badger the nurses about having a tidy up because she was convinced the Queen was coming.

I expected her to be out of theatre about 6pm. I got a text about 9pm, was told to come home in an ominous way and started to fill in the gaps. When I got in my grandad's car at Liverpool Lime Street the next morning he said "So she's got a pretty bad case of cancer." Just how you want that news delivered, but subtlety has never been Buddy's forte. And so started a year of mostly unremarkable cancer treatment, until the last few weeks. Nan reacted fantastically to the first round of chemo and was largely unaffected by the myriad side-effects. Except the hair loss. Which she hated. I told everyone she was in remission, which she would correct. I should have got the hint then. That the tumours were not going away. But she also did not explicitly tell anyone it was terminal so we convinced ourselves it wasn't. Which in some ways was a wonderful gift for us, and in others must be the hugest of burdens for the person saying "Yeah, I'm fine", when they could be like "Gather round me, my darlings, I am dying." That was Barbara, get everyone else settled first. I actively misread her fear and exhaustion in that last fortnight. She was always half in the conversation and now I know why. She was so ill. I remember praising her, like a small child, for forcing down a half bowl of consommé. What a spectacular act of self-delusion to not know what was happening. That her body was just eroding. I feel so frightened to think how much she must have been hurting. And how terrifying and lonely it must have all been, even when she was surrounded by her family. It's unbearable, really. But there she was, pretending it was all not happening to keep us safe. Until one day, animalistically, she realized it was time and asked to be taken to the local hospice for complementary therapy to spare us from living those last, terrible days in a house that we all loved so much. She died there. At 60 years old. With us on all sides. It still feels inconceivable to say. The woman who was so full of life and love and all the things that make a summer afternoon, was just gone. When she was so completely crucial to all of us. And now we had to function without her.

As Completely Fucking Terrible as that all was, I can see it could be more so. My Nana was oldish, beloved, semi-retired and surrounded by the people she valued most. Her period of suffering was relatively short. It was, not surprisingly, quite different to Emma's experience. I can't describe my friend's journey to losing her mum because it's not mine to tell. But I think I can say it was long, acutely painful and defined by a deep sorrow that Berenice carried with her throughout her life. It sounds so lonely and so quiet, for both of them. When I think about her experience, I have an overwhelming compulsion to wrap all my limbs around Emma to warm her with my love, but she'd hate that, so I don't.

And that's us. That's the sad little start to our happy little friendship. It's also time for you to add your loss to the mix. I see her. She sees me. We see you. Let's go rifle through those losses together. What a time we're going to have.

LOSSGISTICS

If most losses are unexpected, how can you possibly know what to expect? We tackle the practical and emotional milestones you might encounter in any given loss.

Emma: How would you explain "Lossgistics" to a layperson?

Robyn: They are the general, recognizable and universal processes around loss.

Emma: Both practical and emotional. And the fundamental thing with Lossgistics is that however and whenever you do them, at some point you are going to have to look at what happened, carve out some time for yourself and let those emotions come out.

Robyn: Yes! You either do a *Grand Designs* where you live in a caravan, work on your emotional house 24/7 for a few months and get it done in a flurry of activity, or you slowly remodel a holiday home at weekends and bank holidays. Either way, you're going to have to rebuild that emotional house, 'cos it's roofless. IT'S ROOFLESS, JONATHAN[1]!

---

1 I don't know who Jonathan is – sorry, Jonathan.

ROBYN ON LOSSGISTICS
Notes from the chaotic extrovert

So here we are, ready to look at the whole loss schtick from opposite angles. I'm the one with the sandwich board and bell, walking around shouting about it. Emma, not so much.

Let me start off by saying, I believe loss is not a problem you solve, it's a journey you have to navigate, which sucks, as I can't give you a cheat sheet. It's also a really long expedition that has no set route, so I can't give you directions either. All I can give you is a map with no coordinates and a reassuring pat on the back. But before you give up, wondering what use a book on loss is when it doesn't walk you through the geography of it all, I'll stop you. Woah there, Sally! We can't give you a treasure map to emotional freedom, but we can give you a brief overview of what you might come across on the way and how you could address these potential obstacles.

We came up with the title of this chapter, "Lossgistics", because we thought it was funny and that's how we handle a good percentage of our trauma, by trying to joke it into normality. The rest of the time is spent with one of us holding the other's hand while we cry in a coffee shop and an awkward waiter lingers, really wanting us to ask for the bill (yes, that waiter is an allegory for society at large). But Lossgistics ARE real. There are processes for loss, whatever that loss is. The first ones are reassuringly straightforward:

1. You will lose something.
2. You will be really fucking sad about it.
3. You will have to perform tedious actions like looking for your hat, finding a new job, returning your ex-friend's stuff or arranging a funeral for your dad.

I'll go through the first milestones as best I can and then we'll come to the larger and more unwieldy topology of general, mid-stage grief (MSG) later. MSG – infinitely less moreish than its catering counterpart but just as likely to give you a headache – is going to be long and, to be honest, less possible to produce a checklist for. As I'm all about measurable problem-solving, I'm dreading it. Might do it as an acrostic poem to leaven things.

1. You will lose something

I'm going to use bereavement as my example form of loss here, and throughout most of the book, as it's the one I know most keenly and the one with the most moving parts. But having done and been privy to the doing of loss[1] I can say, with some degree of confidence, that there's a commonality to all losses. It's a sliding scale. That moment of horror and disbelief is the same (though probably less intense), when you finally articulate the words "My marriage is over," sit down with HR in one of those stony-faced meetings, tell your friend you don't want to be their bridesmaid[2] (or in fact, friend) anymore and realize you can't put those words back in your mouth, or watch the train pull away with your grandmother's umbrella on it.

One of the toughest things to bear in life is that at some point you will lose someone. An actual human person. Someone vital. It might be that you get a call on a July afternoon saying, "Are you sitting down?" and somebody delivers you the worst news of your existence so far. You might get a call on a July afternoon you've sort-of known was coming for months as your loved one was battling a terminal illness. You might get a call on a July afternoon because it was an inevitability that you were

---

1 Because unfortunately it's everywhere.
2 Really happened, including dramatic screaming argument on the South Bank.

always going to lose the person you lost because the world was too much, that their body could never support them, their mind wasn't kind enough to them or society wasn't. There are as many ways of losing someone as there are someones and no one way is easier than the other.

I lost my Nan after a year long struggle with cancer. Though her actual dying was sudden and unexpected. She went into a hospice for a massage and never came out.

We spent so many hours in that place, and by "we" I mean between four and, like, fifteen of us. Everyone was the purest form of themselves. My mum raged. I tried to create schedules to keep everyone under control. Some people insisted on being at her bedside constantly. Others stood in the communal gardens smoking and not saying anything at all. My Nan just asked my Grandad to help her, over and over.

It felt like there were a hundred of us in there when she went. It was only at the point she was satisfied that everyone important had arrived that she allowed herself to go. And we imploded out of the room in a supernova of nervous energy. Or a series of free-floating planets, no longer gravitating around our sun.

2. You will be really fucking sad about it

So the initial sad. The pre-funeral sad. I think if I'm honest, the first few months of sad, at least for me, were not sad at all. They were scared.[3] There is no process the world prepares you for less than death. Apart from, perversely and according to all my reliable sources, motherhood. You will, quite

---

3 Again, I see *you*, I feel that adrenaline as your engagement ring falls down the drain/you sign the divorce papers/you take that contact out of your phone/your parents tell you they plan to sell your childhood home. White hot panic – even if no one died.

probably, have never seen someone pass away and if/when you do it's a hard thing to compute. It's not like on the television. It's primal and frightening and it might be the only thing you'll picture for a while. You might find yourself talking about it constantly like the last scene of a film you can't stop replaying. It's your *Blair Witch Project* moment. You can't figure out why it happened like that, you absolutely don't want to look at it but there it is. Again. You might have lost them in the most peaceful way imaginable, but there's still something completely incomprehensible about seeing a person stop breathing. For a human being to be wholly still. Acknowledge this bit. I'd say that to everyone, even the avoiders. If you found the precise moment you lost your person emotionally insurmountable but don't want to bring it up 'cos no one else seems to, don't worry, everyone else's brains are mouthing "What the fuck?" at them too.

That being said, being with someone as they die isn't something we all experience. In fact, a lot of us don't. I can't deny there is some solace in the inescapable physicality of it all, although some bits I would gladly do without. You can flip it 180 if you're not there because you have so many things you need to know. Whether you just didn't arrive in time. Or you said your goodbyes in advance. Or someone went to sleep and didn't wake up and you were left to process them simply not being around anymore. All equally inconceivable and with gaps in the story that need filling. Were they peaceful? Did they call out for someone? Did a nurse touch their hair or get them water or make sure they weren't scared? Did they know how much you loved them? Continue to the power of infinity. Different kind of terrifying. Different kind of heartbreaking. But same kind of process.

There's no escaping the fact that the global pandemic has thrown in another kind of bereavement too. A loss you actively aren't allowed to be part of. I think, though it's not a competition, this must be the worst of all the ways to lose someone. I can't imagine the pain and confusion that comes with not being *allowed* to be there rather than just, *not* being there. It must be unbearable and frightening in a whole different way and if you have experienced that, I cannot say how sorry I am. Being denied access to that final moment must be torturous. I have also seen friends who have lost parents to suicide and there is no full stop in their story – just a lifetime of questions. Unknotting the threads of any bereavement is nigh on impossible, dealing with it in this context is something else entirely.

However you experience it, it's going to be really bloody tough. And while loss does not automatically result in you developing post-traumatic stress disorder (PTSD), I firmly believe that many of us will suffer with it as a result, whether you're there at the moment your person[4] goes or not. So maybe give that some consideration. Then, after the shock subsides a bit, your heart will just physically ache for them. And it won't stop. Ever. Horror! But it will lessen. You will feel less and less like you're about to go into full cardiac arrest until it's just like a little bruise that throbs when you knock it.

But that's about losing them, what about the bits of you that are lost? If you're like me, your emotional house was built using scaffolding provided by that person. The way you navigated the world was dictated in imperceptible ways by

---

4 Husband/wife/career/friendship/lifestyle/health, etc. I'm Mr Miyagi-ing you here. Wax on and off until you automatically apply my loss to your loss. Crafty, huh…? I'll drop it soon, don't worry.

their impact on you. When you take down the scaffolding of an unfinished house it shifts and certain points bear down so heavily. You'll worry it'll fall as the creaks become more throaty and cracks spiderweb across everything, but if you're lucky, it will settle – precariously and painfully – until you're ready to start building again. It gets better. I promise. It's just unfortunately a full-immersion-of-sad kind of time: sad for the new you without them, sad for the world devoid of their presence, sad for them that they're not in that world anymore. Just a lot of sad.

3. You will have to perform tedious actions like looking for your hat, finding a new job, returning your ex-friend's stuff or arranging a funeral for your dad

Right, straight off the bat, I'm going to admit that I didn't have to do much of this following my bereavement because, despite it being universally acknowledged that I was like a third child to my Nan I am not actually, in the biological sense, a third child so I didn't have to get involved in any of the "deathmin". We've all done those kind of actions with other elements of our lives though: rescued old jumpers off exes, created endless and useless handovers for old jobs, worked out a new way of interacting with your entire family without one key player involved or whatever springs to mind for you: all highly process-driven and if you're like me, in some ways not welcome. But in some ways cleansing and necessary. Complex, isn't it?

Not so with Nan. When she went, I just lay down and did some proper old school languishing – without any need for arranging – rising at noon and napping in the day. I was like a toddler. I could perform very simple tasks and then I'd get weary and need a sit down. And I could. But most people can't. Emma couldn't. She had to actually deal with a funeral, an estate, all the shit stuff. In remote Scotland. In her mid-twenties. I can't imagine it and I wish I could burrow into her brain and extract those bits that she found impossible, but she'd be so mad if I did. Primarily 'cos she wants me to stop trying to fix her stuff all the time, but also, on a practical level, I have very unsteady hands so surgery is not the vocation for me.

There is a comfort in arranging and being distracted, I know from my limited experience and because people have told me so. There's a forward motion and a purpose. You can't nap on that job. There are opportunities to look at a person in context.[5] To think of what was important to them and how they were important to the people around them in turn. To process how to honour that. How to precis their life for the people who didn't know them so well. To think of their favourite flowers, their favourite song. To read poetry and to feel, for a second, understood. To write retrospectively terrible poetry. To buy new tights without ladders for the funeral because they're worth it. To choose their outfit. To choose their *last* outfit. To choose their last outfit based on what can go into a crematorium burner. To choose your outfit. To touch their possessions. To smell them on their clothes again and for a second for them to be there, just off camera. To bathe in them while it feels acceptable and expected to do so. Take a moment in each of these tasks because as shit as they are, they can be an odd kind of meditation. You'll look back and be grateful for the way they served you and the discoveries you made, that there was a structure to your grief before it becomes this amorphous salty

---

5 Or place, thing, moment-in-time, hope, wish, situation, denim jacket, family home etc etc. You don't have to have a funeral for all these things but if it helps, you do you, boo.

blancmange you can't really get a hold of (it's a blancmange of tears, if you're wondering what I'm imagining there).

What comes next...

Once those three key benchmarks are achieved, or are at least underway, most bets are off, I'm afraid. You might look for distractions to avoid the way you feel, or ways to validate it. You might wear your grief like your team football strip or pop it in a box. It will evolve. It will diminish. As it fades into the background and stops taking up your plane of vision you will get a sense of its shape and what to do with it. Do what you feel is right but do make sure that what *you* feel is right is also healthy. Get some therapy, because your therapist is a great person to say, "Manuel, shoplifting is thrilling and a lovely way to take your mind off the collapse of your haulage firm but let's look at the wider ramifications of that petty crime", while drinking a green tea and engaging you in the game of competitive endurance staring they all seem to learn at Therapy Camp.[6] Note to self, [insert name]: you already know the unhealthy thing isn't right but it makes you feel good – just do your due diligence and check it's not going to kill you.

Following my loss, two people said things that were useful to me and I'll share them with you now. If you're a person who can't cope without someone managing your expectations, these will be gold. If you aren't, they are going to bum you out hard. My friend Shell came to see me a few weeks after my Nan passed away. She was basically the only person I knew who had lost someone significant at that age so I pumped her for info. She said this: "You are going to be

6 We know access to therapy can be variable depending on an endless range of factors. That's simply not right. Head to our *Help Is Out There* section for a few pointers on how to get the help *you* need.

Giant of lakead

really fucking sad for a really long time." Yeah, direct, isn't it? But in a world where your biggest fear is probably that you'll feel this unbearably miserable forever, hearing someone saying, "I see this is unbearable and unfortunately, it's going to be like that for a while, but, crucially, not for the rest of time", is such a relief. It's like going from being David Blaine in that plastic box over the Thames, watching people walk by with no serviceable route back to them to, well… being two people in that plastic box over the Thames equipped with a key and a countdown clock. Hopefully the jazzy clock from actual *Countdown*.

A woman who I worked with for a month, who had lost her dad, told me that for the first two years I would not be myself. She was right, too. It was a period of adjustment. I exhibited a series of boringly predictable destructive behaviours. I was me but with all the most extreme facets. Maybe because feeling things could be so difficult or so unruly I had to feel them all To The Max. These were my glory years of grief – I slotted all the most out-there behaviour in and absolutely luxuriated in it. I inhabited it completely. My Ziggy Stardust period. When I didn't know who I was it gave me a purpose, a USP, a bejewelled catsuit of a coping strategy replete with a ginger mullet of woe.

But somewhere along the way I stripped off the very involved costume, shoes, accessories, wig and face paint combo and started just being Robyn again. Robyn 2.0. Very much not the same but someone who could make room for other things gradually. Circumstances changed and as they did, I did too, and I could shed little bits of the persona I'd created, and work on the damaging behaviours so I was more functional and less, well, sad.

What have I learnt? Trust that the general onward trajectory of your life should help. Life *will* move in a forward direction, time *will* tick on and you *will* just start to heal. Don't forget loss can be a passive thing too. Think of it like a big scab – you can't "think" a big scab healed, there is an element of just knowing that your body will take care of it. Savlon it and wait it out. You'll feel the compulsion to pick at it less and less because the initial, overwhelming itch will subside. It is very gradual. There'll be a scar but you won't have a huge open wound, won't that be nice!

One day, without realizing what you're doing, you'll pick up a brick and absent-mindedly pop it in your emotional house. And then another. And then another. And then maybe a non-load-bearing wall will fall down and you'll be like, "What the fuck?", but don't panic. The whole bloody house nearly collapsed, remember? That wall obviously had some fundamental weaknesses and needed to be rebuilt. You know you've got the skills to rebuild it. You've got the skills to do the whole lot. That's where I come – very briefly 'cos there's a whole chapter on it later – to why a loss *can*, in some ways, make you better. It made me better, because it made me realize that if the worst thing I could have imagined happening had happened and if I wasn't dragged under by it, then I could make it through most things. Because crap things seemed to keep happening in my childhood, in my teens and early twenties, I had fashioned myself a kick-ass Marvel persona – *Cursed Girl: doomed to have absolute shit happen to her always*. But then the worst did. And like Peter Parker when Uncle Ben died, I eventually became a better Spiderman. What a thrilling start to this tell-all autobiography: *Robyn Donaldson: I am actually Spiderman*. But you get my point. You will be a different person dealing with loss five years in than five days in. You will hopefully have a handle on it and, if you're that way out, you can repackage it to be something that actively helps you. There's a reason there are so many loss organizations, and it's not just altruism. Giving your loss a purpose means it wasn't for nothing and that is a powerful thing. You don't have to set up a loss organization. That's an extreme example. But the marathon runners, the car boot stallers, the bake sale bakers? All that on a smaller scale. Making loss work for them.

So there you go, no to-do list (apart from the one opposite), no advice on how to skip steps and fast-forward to feeling absolutely normal again, but hopefully a little insight into how it might go down when everything can feel a bit overwhelmingly unknowable.

ACTION STATIONS
Ways to help yourself and everybody else.

- Here's a tasty little tip you probably already know: being of assistance can be helpfully distracting. That's why I've made enough tea in my life to fill Lake Windermere, but any offer of aid allows you to refocus on the wider world for a minute.

- Allocate time for grief. Book in points in your day/week/month to re-examine and stop getting into an avoidance cycle. This could be in a formal way, as per below, or it could be just sitting-and-thinking time. It could be a colouring book of pictures of the thing you lost (the kind of which the internet now allows you to order). Just set the intention of regularly looking at whatever's got you hurting.

- Take steps to find a professional to talk to. I should have got therapy early on. I could have dealt with the PTSD and maybe avoided some of the ongoing anxiety I've experienced since. Even if it's only for a few sessions, give it a go. It might not be for you but it's unlikely you'll feel more bereaved because you went to counselling.

START TO

HEAL.

LIFE WILL MOVE IN A FORWARD

YOU WILL JUST

TIME WILL TICK ON AND

DIRECTION,

EMMA ON LOSSGISTICS
Notes from the anxious introvert

And now for the flip-side of Lossgistics, from me, Emma, the one who tried to look in the opposite direction and hoped it would all go away. Spoiler: it didn't. It made it worse, and, with hindsight, I probably could've done with taking a leaf or two out of Robyn's book. As you'll have gleaned from the intro, the two of us don't have very much in common when it comes to loss, but we've both said that it would've been really helpful if somebody had told us what to expect from it. Because many losses – whether it's the death of a loved one or mourning another part of life entirely – share so many of the same processes. And where Robyn moved through those processes in an outward-facing symphony of self-expression, I shut the doors and put a broom through the handles. Because public loss chat to somebody like me feels like nude dancing on prime-time television with everybody I've ever met watching – uncomfortable. I've done a lorra lorra therapy and worked really hard (on the loss, not the dancing) but it is, as they say, a process. And not the fun, spreadsheet kind (just me?), but the cleaning-the-oven kind that you put off until it's absolutely, inescapably bad.

I once told my therapist that it felt like the world was shit and it was always going to be like that, and I think that's how loss feels sometimes, whether it's the loss of a person, possession or personal freedom. Like an insurmountable cliff face you don't want to climb but have to. My therapist, who is a very wise woman, replied that unfortunately, I was right – life might always feel shit, unless I continued to work on making it not feel like that. And, damn it, she was right. So I'm here to tell you that, whatever loss you're going through and however you're dealing with it right now, change *is* possible and more often than not, necessary, to get to the other side and feel at peace.

The thing about loss is that it sucks. Sucks big time, like a high-quality vacuum cleaner. And no matter how much you fortify yourself against it, the likelihood is that it's going to hurt to some degree, ranging from a wistful sigh to a 40-year wailing marathon. See, I think we make ourselves a little emotional nest in life, feathering it with the people, places and things that hold us up; the walk you take in a field every morning before the day starts; the friend who's got your back; the job you always knew you wanted. These things are part of our identity and our support system – part of who we've made ourselves in the world. So when the field burns down in a freak accident, the friend ghosts you or you're suddenly made redundant, it hurts. This thing, person, or place that was always just *there,* isn't. And it's a shock. In fact, I reckon there's usually one big initial shock, followed by lots of other smaller shocks. Like an earthquake. Yes, let's say that: loss is like an earthquake that shakes your little emotional nest, potentially to smithereens, while, if you're anything like me, you sit watching from behind a curtain, hoping nobody notices you shedding a tear.

Don't be a clam

Let's get this said: any loss is shocking. Even if you expect it to happen, plan it in, have a signed legal document stating that it will happen on a certain date, and a man follows you around everywhere with a loud speaker, announcing that it's going to happen, it will still come as a shock to be suddenly without something. My Mum was sick for a long time before she died, but I was in no way prepared for her to be gone. Even now, I still have a micro-shock when I move to pick up the phone and call her, only to realize she's not there. But the actual thing, I think, often looks nothing like we think it's going to. In some ways, probably better and in some ways, probably worse. For me, it was both. I thought life would end and it didn't (better), and I thought I'd be able to grieve for her freely, but I very much didn't (worse). There's so much about loss that nobody tells you beforehand, and, though all loss shares some common traits, each experience is utterly unique. That's why knowing what to expect from your loss can be so tricky. But not impossible, I promise.

It all starts – as does everything in life – with you, dear reader. With who you are. The kind of person you are – and the way you operate in the world – will determine how you respond to loss and how the people around you respond to your loss as well. The premise of this book is that all grief looks different, which is great and empowering and yada yada, but it's also about the fact that recognizing grief in other people who don't do it like you do it, can be hard. So use this section on yourself and on your nearest and dearest. I think understanding the kind of person you (and they) are can make the world of difference. And, because I love to over-simplify things, I'm gonna say that you can work a lot of this out by knowing whether the loss-ee is an introvert or an extrovert. Received wisdom would have us think that introverts are shy and extroverts are confident; that introverts are antisocial loners, while extroverts love people. And, although there are personality traits that lend themselves to this idea, it's less about sociability and more about energy processing. If this were a shampoo advert, I'd be about to show you some floating diagrams of science. Let's say your

Loss sucks like a high-quality vacuum cleaner.

energy levels are a battery at half-charge. An extrovert will walk into a room full of people and their energy battery will be charged up even higher by the human contact. An introvert could walk into that same room and their battery would be drained by the energy expended in it. The extrovert needs people and contact for energy, the introvert needs the opposite: time alone to piece back together and recharge. If you're not sure which one you are, there's an easy test that I use on myself:

Let's say you've had a terrible, terrible day; you're sad inside, your boss yelled at you, you missed the bus and you tore your jacket on a nail. A friend gets in touch to see whether you fancy a meet-up later – is your first thought:

A Yes, thank goodness, I need to get some of this stress off my chest.

B Euuuurgh, please don't make me – all I want to do is go home.

If you answered A, you probably see the meet-up as a chance to bond, connect and charge back up after a draining day – all extrovert qualities. And if you answered B, like me, you see the meet-up as yet another thing you have to use your energy to get through – that's some introvert thinking. Of course, it's not that simple – you get introverts with extrovert tendencies and extroverts with introvert tendencies and so on and so forth, but as a starting point for working out how you might deal with loss, it can be a really helpful thing to be aware of. There's maximum power in understanding what kind of a griever you are, and it might be fully, heartbreakingly, bone-crushingly, awfully sad while you get to know yourself better, but on the other side of that grief bridge is a whole new relationship with yourself, the world and the thing you lost.

It can also be useful to take a look at how loss was presented to you as a kid. Lots of us have experienced hamster-loss, some of us will have experienced other kinds – maybe your family relocated and you lost the familiar life you knew, or perhaps like Robyn one parent left and your world turned upside down. Whatever the loss, the attitudes of the people around us can massively impact how we express ourselves, and that's never truer than when we're growing up, learning about the world and setting our behaviours. Personally, I come from a long line of people who do their thinking and feeling on the inside, and outward emotional expression hasn't been my family's forte. So when my Grandad (my Mum's dad) died, I was protected from the difficult truth. I wasn't allowed to visit him in hospital towards the end, I wasn't allowed to go to the funeral and I never saw anybody crying about it. If they did, I was whisked out of the room before a tear could form. It was all deemed Too Sad and therefore off-limits to a child. But children are little sponges who soak up everything you're giving them, whether they understand it or not. So, was it the right thing to do? I think in grief and sadness there is no right or wrong, but looking back on those moments really helps me to re-frame my loss-needs not as difficult and unexplainable weirdness, but as a set of learned behaviours. We are the sum total of our life's experiences, and – though it might be tempting to give yourself a hard time for not getting through a loss in the pseudo agreed-upon format – there's really no need.

Live the moment

When we think about loss, it tends to go something like this: person loses something, person is sad, person feels better, person is OK. But it absolutely does not always look like that. In fact, I think it very rarely does, at least for the person going through it. It's rarely the poetic, staring-out-of-a-rainy-window situation we see in movies, and I've never once experienced loss that felt like song lyrics told me it would. In fact, in my experience, it's been less "loss, sad, better, OK" than it has: "loss, pretend everything's fine, take it all out on yourself, develop some mental health issues, have problematic relationships, grind yourself down to nothing, job-hop, worry a lot, do lots of shopping, worry some more, stop sleeping," etc. Until you finally start to work through it and decide to write a book.

The moment you go through loss; the split second in time when you go from having to not-having might be too painful for you to look at straight away, and that's OK. Depending on your emotional make-up, it might take you days, weeks or even years before you can look at it. And if you need to take time, that's for you to decide. Everybody's experiences of loss are different, and there's no right or wrong way to deal with it. So long as at some point you're able to face the reality of what's happening, don't let anybody rush you to feel or act in any way. It's why we called this book *It's Your Loss*, because it is.

Once the initial punch in the loss-gonads has been dealt, there's usually some form of admin to be taken care of. This is the bit lots of us find really hard, because it places you squarely at the centre of the very thing you hope most to avoid looking at. Maybe there's a funeral to organize or a will to look through; maybe you need to start job hunting or go to court or – I don't know – raise a child, but loss often comes with a paper trail, and it can be a hard reminder that the rest of the world has not stopped because you are sad. Some people relish the structure and the planning; I hated everybody involved for not feeling what I was feeling inside. Both are valid. I was really active in other ways, like obsessively clearing out my wardrobe, and when you're that way inclined, from the outside it probably looks like you're getting on fine and moving forwards in a positive direction when in fact you're moving sort of diagonally across a floor of knives, with no shoes on. Whatever you do, try not to follow my example, which was to look the other way, bury my head in the sand and pretend it wasn't happening. It led to me being taken advantage of and missing out on a lot of the keepsakes I would've loved to have kept as a reminder of my Mum. So, here's what I'll say: if you can't look at it, ask somebody else to look at it for you. If there are forms to be filled in, jobs to be hunted, or calls to be made and you feel like you're not up to it, you gotta ask for help. Even if somebody just sits with you while you do it, this is the moment to reach out and ask for support. Because the world does not stop turning, and the only person missing out while you look the other way, is you.

Then comes the great re-joining. Unless you make for the hills to live in a cave with a stick for a best friend, there will come a point in your loss when you'll probably need to go back and re-join real life. I know – gross. There's something wholly disconcerting about real things when somebody pulled the normality rug from under your feet, and the first time you go to the shops or head back into the office you'll probably feel like a bruised peach. A little shell-shocked, a little sad, a little embarrassed that everybody knows your business, or even a little annoyed that they don't. I remember looking around my office and thinking nobody knows I have this giant lake of sad inside me. It can feel like a really lonely time, especially if you're young. Because, although we all like to chirp about how loss doesn't have a timeline, to the world at large, it kind of does. There'll come a point when people just sort of expect you to be OK again. The cards stop coming, the sympathy flowers have died, friends stop asking you about it over lunch, and you're cast adrift in a big old world, without that part of your emotional nest. Although it's tempting to assume this means you need to get on with it, and that you're weird for still having these overwhelming feelings of sadness, I'm here to tell you to very much not do that, and, if you can, to seek out connection with your emotions, either through therapy, support groups or something solo like journaling. It's not always convenient to be long-term grief-stricken in a world that demands you are always on, but if you're sad, you're sad, and that has to come out some way. People can only work with what you give them, so, rather than presenting a big smile to everybody because you think that's what they want, it's OK to let them know you're still going through it. It doesn't need to be a big conversation, but a little mention to say that you're struggling, even if you're not showing it – there isn't a good friend or boss in the world who wouldn't appreciate being let in on that.

Speaking of good friends, it's worth saying that depending on who you have in your life and what sort of person you are, a time of loss can leave you very vulnerable, not just to emotions, but to people with less-than-good intentions. While your brain is a mush of wet tissue and glue and you're busy trying to distract yourself from the brand new gaping hole in your life, try to take a second now and again to look at how your relationships are working for you. Part of me crumbled inside when my Mum died, and there were people in my life who took advantage of that, seeing me not as somebody who was grieving and needing support, but as somebody who was weak and could be exploited. And if ever you've been in a problematic relationship, you'll know how easy it is to let them, in part because it distracts you and in part, possibly, because you feel like it's what you deserve. From a distance now, I can see what was happening in my situation and why it happened, but with your nose pressed up against the glass, it isn't always easy, so I'm going to encourage you to look at the relationships that are causing you anxiety or making you feel less than worthy of support and love, and, even if you can't change them right now, to be aware of how they're affecting you, and give yourself time to process that too.

You do you

If you're like me, every loss you live through – from the jobs you lose to the loved ones who die, to the friendships you no longer have – will feel messy and uncomfortable and you'll want to get out of feeling that way as quickly as possible. And that's OK. It's not nice to feel not-nice. But running away from stuff is exhausting, so finding ways to sit with sadness, rather than pretending it isn't there, and trying not to hold on too hard to what you think of as normality – that's the goal. As introverts, we have to learn that when we're hurting, the world needs to go away. Then loss becomes more about turning the gaze inwards, having a look at your reaction to it, feeling the feelings as they come and having lots of time to do it in. Maybe you'll have creative outlets like writing or journaling, maybe you'll want to be close to things that remind you of what you lost. Maybe both, maybe neither; maybe you'll want one thing one time and be repulsed by it another. See, grief for anything is an evolution. It changes with you over time, and can be whatever you need it to be. It's an expression of the love you had for that person, thing or time you're missing. And if it hurts real bad, that's the counterbalance to the amazing good bits you had when they were around. So don't be afraid. Feel it, hold it dear, because it's yours, and there's something strangely wonderful about that.

ACTION STATIONS

When you think you need to be an island, how do you find support?

- Think about asking somebody for help and notice how that makes you feel. Was your gut response anger? Fear? Whatever it was, make a mental note and – if you can – write it down and explore that feeling to try and understand it.

- Try asking somebody for something reeeeally small today – it could be, "Can you help me remember that song we used to love dancing to?" or it could be, "Please may I have my favourite jacket back?" Once you get more comfortable asking for small things, the big things will get easier.

- If you really feel unable to ask for help, and have an overwhelming to-do list, schedule in short, manageable periods of Doing Stuff time and follow them up with some kind of luxurious treat time, to make everything feel better.

Dr Sheetal Says...

Loss is a journey. We will all navigate this road differently. This journey is not linear and you will struggle to piece together a trajectory on day one which will look the same at the end. Some are on this journey for a long time and many take some time to understand what they are looking for. For others, their version of grief ending may be that they are able to carry on with life with an acceptance that the loss has occurred, and being OK with that. The circumstances of the loss will play a role too. Could I have done more to help? Did I have a hand in this eventuality? If only I was there. I should have spent more time with them. Now they will never know how much I loved them. These are all questions that are normal, valid and important to work through and reframe.

It can be easy to internalize other people's expectations (especially when you are feeling vulnerable or unsure of yourself), and you can feel the sense of pressure, weakness or even defectiveness for *still* going through inner turmoil after a certain amount of time has passed. Why can't *I* deal with it but others can? But if everyone else is hiding their sadness too, we can't truly know how they are really coping, can we? This is why it's so important to speak and be open when you're ready, not only to show vulnerability to your friends and teach yourself that it's OK, but also to change the world's perspective on how it makes people feel they *should* be coping.

The importance of talking

If we acknowledge our anxieties and losses, growth and resilience will be more significant. As therapists, we *know* that talking and sharing can really help... we witness this all the time. After most first sessions I hear from my clients how much easier it was to talk than they expected and also how cathartic it was. Generally people come to see us because there has been a realization that in whatever way they were coping up until now, it is clearly no longer working for them. Maybe that process has served its purpose and you are ready to admit that.

A couple of things to consider...

- What would I do if it was my best friend, sister, partner? Would I want them to feel that they could come to me no matter what?

- Something I often ask my clients is, "How do you want to feel, be, or cope with this stuff down the line, and how do we work towards that together?"

"I spent most of the spring after the birth of my son in bed. I was recovering from postpartum psychosis and a two-week stay in a psychiatric facility. By the time I was released, I felt like I'd been blown apart, and I was no longer sure of who I was.

I fell into a deep depression, it was as though someone had tied an anchor to my body, and there was only darkness. My son was six months old, but I couldn't stand to touch him. Somewhere I knew that I wasn't being a good mother, but I couldn't begin to feel anything about it.

We moved into a flat with windows facing the south sun, and my husband bought a pink rug and yellow cushions, as though the brightness could find a way within.

My memory of that spring is sitting in the sunshine and only feeling an aching pain, as though my body no longer wanted me to inhabit it. And all I could do was to try, to keep going, and hope that one day the light would come in.

Everyone told me that it would, and I tried to believe them, even though I couldn't imagine it. But it did, slowly, glimmers at first, and then longer moments. The world became clearer, the light brighter, and I could touch my son without flinching.

I try not to mourn those days, to think about what was lost. Instead I think about how desperately I wished to get better, and how grateful I am that I found my way back."

Catherine Cho, author of *Inferno: A Memoir of Motherhood and Madness*, on her experiences of early motherhood

THE UNMISTAKABLE WHIFF OF GUILT, ANGER, ANXIETY (AND THE REST...)

Why, when you're going through a loss, does everything else feel so bloody hard? A two-person romp through all the other complicated emotion stuff a loss can throw up.

Emma: I think that's the thing nobody really tells you – you're never just sad, you're one million other things too.

Robyn: It's like everything is massively heightened. Someone cranked up all the dials.

Emma: Yes, and your brain is always going to look for the path of least resistance. So whatever stops it feeling like the world is imploding, it'll do, even if that replacement thing is AWFUL.

Robyn: I think it cleared a lot of the emotional baggage I'd been lugging around from my childhood, because that didn't matter. I found a lot of perspective in that loss.

Emma: Like a cleansing, controlled bushfire.

Robyn: Yep, you see the real landscape. I think I was immediately much heavier with it, but after the grief fug went away I was lighter – what about you?

Emma: Oh, mine was like a heavy weight that compacted all my other issues. I really had to force it into the emotional box, which was already full. So then to take the lid off would have been a disaster.

EMMA ON THE UNMISTAKABLE WHIFF OF GUILT, ANGER, ANXIETY (AND THE REST...)

Notes from the guilty, anxious one

Experiencing loss is rarely just experiencing loss. You know when you try to get a clothes hanger out of a bag of other clothes hangers? However hard you try, you never just get one. You'll probably end up angry and sweaty and cursing the person who made clothes hangers a thing. And loss is the same. Losing something or somebody might happen as an event all on its own, but it'll almost always bring with it a whole bunch of emotional things you weren't expecting. If you're built like me and like to keep a lid on the old emotional box where possible, that can be a hideously unwelcome discovery. Or, if like me, you're hell-bent on not looking at the loss in question, it can become a hideously effective coping mechanism you'll spend many years later unpicking.

Of course, it all starts waaaaay before you actually go through a loss. Often, these things are so baked into who we are, we don't even know they're there. If somebody asked you what kind of person you are, what would you say? Confident, needy, sad, anxious, No.1 Wham! fan...? Are you prone to bouts of depression? Do you have an online shopping habit that just won't quit? Maybe you have OCD or can't stop buying cats? Maybe you're hyper-organized and have a spreadsheet for everything; a work-obsessed power-player who's in the office at 5am and still there at midnight. You might be a finger-picker, or a lip-biter; a serial partier or an hermetic recluse. It's worth having a think about because whoever you were before the loss lorry hit you, is going to have some bearing on how you deal with that loss.

69

We're creatures of habit. Our brains don't like change. So, when we're in shock after any kind of loss, those brains are going to reach for the nearest thing that feels familiar and helpful, even if that thing is very much not helpful, long-term. So, the online shopper funnels deeper and deeper into ordering stuff (surely, the ultimate distraction?), the workaholic takes on every project in sight and moves a bed into the office, the finger-picker's thumbs are red raw and bleeding. We all have unhelpful emotional behaviours, crutches and coping mechanisms – they're a symptom of living in the world and finding ways to navigate adversity without falling apart – and you betcha sweet bippy[1] that when you're at your most vulnerable is when they'll start to really creep in. So, while your brain's busy dealing with the Big Disaster, things you might usually be vigilant against – like stress, debt, addiction, unhealthy relationships, or lack of self-care – are free to romp all over your emotional garden, unchecked. Because, when you're bereft; when you're focused on a Terrible Thing, your defences are down. Your energy is low. Your resistance is weak. And your lovely brain, which just wants to protect you, calls in reinforcements from the last time you felt like this. Only, those things aren't always the best things for you. So you're sad. But you can't focus on the sad because your brain's all like, "Look at this terrible memory from ten years ago!" or, "Remember when you fit into those jeans?" or, "I wonder what your awful ex is doing with their new partner on Instagram..." or, "You know what's fun? DRINKING!" You see where this is going? None of those have anything to do with your loss, and you might not even feel like they're connected when they come

---

1 This is something my Mum used to say – let's bring it back.

up, but they're all your brain's roundabout way of helping out with the threat – your loss – by switching your attention away from it and onto something else.

Of course, it rarely works. You can't just switch off your emotions about one thing – wouldn't it be easier if we could? A selective emotional fuse board where we could just pop the switches off when we need to? When we decide to switch off the bit that deals with the loss experience, we trip the system, everything goes dark, and we generally stop processing anything at all. And then you find yourself a decade later unable to sit still by yourself for five minutes because the bad thoughts come in. Just me? Your way of avoiding might look different to mine, but ultimately, not dealing with the Big Thing can be really damaging, and doesn't help in the long term, unless you love feeling on edge for the rest of eternity. For quiet people like me, it's about finding ways to be firm but kind to yourself through the loss, build out the space and time and structures to focus on it, understand it, and eventually work through it. Sounds good, right?

The best at being bad

I'm the master of guilt. If turning things which I have no control over into something that's All My Fault were an Olympic sport, I'd win all the gold medals. They'd have to invent a bigger gold medal just for me. Even things that are done *to* me will turn out – in my head – to be my fault. So, when I lost my Mum, there was a whole lot of guilt thrown into the mix, that continued long into my grieving process. And I'm here to tell you that if I – the guilt, anxiety and not-looking-after-yourself sensei – can learn to look objectively at these things, it's highly likely that you can find a way to do it too.

We can't
give you a
treasure map
to emotional
freedom

Let's talk learned coping mechanisms. I'd been fearing losing my Mum since I was little. As she pulled away from dropping me off at my Dad's house, I'd start praying she wouldn't die in a car crash on the way home – that sort of thing. In retrospect, after many years of therapy, I can see that that in itself was an early symptom of anxiety – my brain's little way of exerting control and protecting me against nasty surprises. And if you too have been worrying about something happening that actually does then happen, you'll know it means that you feel that you've been proven right. Those years of being afraid and all that secret worrying have borne fruit and you were correct to have been preparing yourself for it. For me, these weren't articulated thoughts as much as they were just a base-level understanding of how the world worked. Fear keeps you safe. Fear is your friend. Always listen to fear. And then, two things happened: first, I couldn't think about the fact that she was gone. And it was such an overwhelmingly huge thing in such a young life that my brain had to call in the big guns to stop me focusing on it. Enter the second thing: anxiety. Chest-clamping, nerve-shaking, insomnia-inducing anxiety. Now I knew fear protected me, I could be fearful about everything. I believed I needed to keep everybody around me happy or they'd leave me, so I'd run myself ragged going out, having dinners, attending work parties and birthdays, staying up late talking with friends and bending over backwards to keep a terrible relationship going. I was constantly thinking about who I thought other people needed me to be, rather than what I could do for myself. I tried to cut out social events where people might ask about it, but couldn't spend time on my own. I tried to sit still, but fidgeted constantly. I tried to distract myself, and would do things in a frenzy, like throwing out all my clothes or organizing the spice cupboard. I'd make myself comfort food then just sit and look at it. I'd have coffee for breakfast and an apple for dinner. I'd be on my phone, watching TV, shopping, doing, always on. It was anything to keep my mind active; anything I could worry about became a monolith on my horizon, and the best worry of all was that I was not good enough. That I was bad. If I believed that things were my fault, I could chastise myself. I could believe that improving myself would make me feel better. It's a form of mental self-harm that I indulged in with wild abandon. Does any of it sound familiar? This is all the hairy drain sludge that came out of the plughole of my loss, but yours could look completely different. I know people who feel acute rage; people who need to create; people who need to give back. Not all side-effects of loss are terrible, but it helps to be able to spot the ones that are, because, when they're recurring behaviours, you can start to watch out for the early warning signs.

Guilt feels like a good starting point, because for lots of us it forms part of our journey through loss, and indeed is one of the famous seven stages of grief (the others being shock and denial, pain and guilt, anger and bargaining, depression, reflection and loneliness, the upward turn and acceptance). In my case, guilt pops up a lot, because believing everything's all my fault gives me something to feel anxious about, and that is my ultimate way of not dealing with things. I'll give you an example that looks at a loss that isn't death, but estrangement. I'm estranged from my step-dad, for very valid reasons backed up by my own experiences and other people's. And yet still, there's a little tap-tap-tapperoo at my emotional windows and it's Old Man Guilt at the door, here to tell me that I've got it all wrong. That I'm overreacting –

that he is old now and might be sad inside and that I'm hurting him by not being present. Luckily, I have a very sensible therapist to remind me what purpose that guilt serves: to make me feel bad, keep me in my well-worn emotional state and stop me from changing and growing. Because movement into the unknown can feel more frightening than staying where we are, even if that place is terribly painful. But if you can work into understanding those feelings, that growth can gently plop you out into the world a happier, more robust version of yourself.

Hindsight is a wonderful thing

Often, we have no control over when losses happen, or even what feels like a loss to us. A seemingly joyful occasion can leave us mourning the life and identity we feel is being taken away. So a prosperous retirement might end up feeling like loss of direction and purpose; a successful graduation means leaving your student life behind. In my own life, often when I've had positive milestones, they're followed by an acute sense of loss – a hollow where the build-up to that milestone had been. And when that happens – when it feels like the world thinks you ought to be rejoicing – there's a special kind of loneliness tied up with it all. A sort of unnameable shame when you feel like your reaction to something is at odds with the way everybody else seems to feel about it. In fact, for people-pleasing folks, that can be a key thing: feeling like your reaction to loss has anything to do with other people. When my Mum died, I was at pains to make everything OK for everybody else, and if you're anything like me you might feel the same. The desire to not be a burden, not be over-sad, not attract too much attention, to make everything seem OK – it's a coping mechanism, and one that served *me* well enough for a while, in that I was able to function as a human being in the world. But of course, constantly pretending something isn't an issue takes a whole lot of energy. Worrying all the time will really take it out of you, and eventually you might just burn out and *won't* be able to function in the world as a human being. Once you know that your brain defaults to a certain reaction when there's something you need to deal with, though, you can try learning to do the opposite. To actively try to process and not rush yourself to do it. I talk about anxiety and fear as my example reactions because they're familiar to me, but yours might be anger, or hyperactivity, or feelings of depression, or intricate kitchen filing systems. Maybe have a think about where your head goes when you get stressed. It's pretty uncomfortable, but – like physical exercise – the only way to build mental strength and fortitude is to train yourself to be OK with that.

It's easy to think of coping mechanisms as just the way you're built. They're so much part of who we are that questioning them can feel really threatening. Your brain's developed them to protect you against the big bad world, like an emotional zorb as you tumble down the rocky hill of life. Take away the zorb and that tumble feels a lot more dangerous, much more naked and probably quite frightening. But actually, although while standing at the top of the hill you'll imagine the cuts and grazes and broken bones, what actually happens when you take away the zorb is that you learn to run down the hill. You teach yourself where to confidently place each foot – you learn to trust yourself to get up when you fall. And you realize that if you do take a bad fall and break your face, it'll be OK, because your face will heal, and you might even get brand new veneers as a result. (In this analogy let's say veneers are shiny, white pearls of knowing yourself a little bit better.)

Like training – and definitely zorbing – sometimes it's best to engage the help of a professional so you don't fracture your leg the first time you try. For example, I got myself to the point that I couldn't think about my Mum or look at photos without having some kind of panic attack. In fact, those panic attacks had started to creep into my everyday, so I found myself a therapist to talk to; and if things are tough for you, if you feel out of control or just feel a bit weird lots of the time, I can't recommend it enough. Find a therapist, find a group – find somebody outside of yourself who you can go to for level-headed intel when you need it. And if anxiety's your reaction of choice, try following an anxious thought to its absolute worst conclusion. Allow me to demonstrate with one of my own go-to wormholes.

Emma: I don't want to take on this freelance job.
Brain: But the client really wants you to.
Emma: Yeah, I guess so.
Brain: And you don't want to let them down...
Emma: No, you're right.
Brain: Because they've given you work in the past...
Emma: Mmmmhmmmm.
Brain: And you don't want to seem ungrateful.
Emma: No, that's true, I don't.
Brain: You've taken quite a while to respond to their email – I bet they're really mad at you.
Emma: Oh no, do you think so?
Brain: Yeah, I bet they think you're really unprofessional.
Emma: Oh man... I'm just not sure I have the time...

Brain: But you could make the time. You really need the money.

Emma: I mean...

Brain: What if no other work comes in for ages?

Emma: I guess...

Brain: You'll have to live off your tax money and then you'll get done by HMRC and won't be able to pay your rent and you'll have to move out and your business will die and your partner will leave you and you'll never work again because the whole industry will know you've failed.

Yeah, my brain is a dick, but you can see that that one little anxiety about whether to take on a little freelance job actually carries with it the much bigger fear of total loss of everything I own and love in the world. Rather than try to tamp down that initial spike of fear and tell ourselves we're being silly, how about knowing that if we allow the fear to take shape, and follow the thought to the end of the road, it'll often turn out that we're giving a very small thing a large amount of projected meaning.

When I first started seeing my therapist, hoping to be cured of anxiety, she told me that I might never be completely anxiety-free, but that with work, one day I could learn to view it as a slightly embarrassing old friend who I don't really need to have around anymore, and that's the hope I have for you and any unhelpful emotional coping mechanisms you might have, too. That one day you'll see them not as a looming presence on your loss journey, but more like an over-protective, neurotic friend who you might wave to across the road, and then wander down a side street so you don't have to say hello to. I know, the first time I heard that

I inwardly scoffed and thought, absolutely no way, mate. But – in my case at least – my therapist was right. With time and effort and a bit of self-love, that emotional sludge that comes up with your loss can start to pare back. You may well discover the drain unblocker that is knowing it's OK to feel terrified, to communicate that you're terrified. To sit with that fear and explore it. Because loss is frightening. It's uncharted territory that you're exploring, often by yourself. And though it's hard and uncomfortable and spiky and raw, through it is hope and promise and rebuilding. It's OK to focus on it. It's OK to feel bad. But it's also OK to ask for help and to start feeling better about it – you don't have to continue to feel bad for the loss to have meant something. Ultimately, if you let it, loss can be your superpower. Your empathy-making, self-loving journey to a comfortable life. I believe it because I've lived it, and I know you can too.

ACTION STATIONS

When you're feeling overwhelmed, how can you lend yourself a hand?

- Try to focus on the facts, not your fears about those facts, to stop yourself spiralling. Write them down if you can.

- Carve out time in your day or your week to be alone and focus on "the thing". You could go for a walk, book in a therapy session, run a bath or sit and journal – whatever works for you.

- If you know you're prone to certain behaviours like online shopping or drinking too much, keep the action of the behaviour, but do it lite. So you might do online window shopping and not actually hit buy now, or pour yourself a tonic, but not add the gin. Sometimes it's just the distraction we're craving.

ROBYN ON THE UNMISTAKABLE WHIFF OF GUILT, ANGER, ANXIETY (AND THE REST...)

Notes from the guilty, anxious, and – crucially – angry one

I'm going to give you the absolute opposite standpoint, of course. I'm doing loss in a full ballgown, on the bow of a ship, screaming into the wind while someone records and airs it (hopefully globally). I am big and public, bombastic and direct. I am the anti-Emma. So here's my completely black and white, uncompromising take on it. I don't think grief is a thing you do. I think the verb "to grieve" is utterly misleading. Because often what you're doing is feeling a staggering number of emotions, all in a randomized order and in very quick succession. And then feeling Absolutely Nothing. Before feeling all the feelings again. Think of it like a high-stakes emotional tombola – ultimate chaos with peaks of pure joy and abject misery.

Loss, to me, is about looking at something in retrospect, thinking, "That was wonderful – I really should have appreciated that more," and then compulsively examining every facet of it. Whether that's your human nan, the ace job you jacked in or that really excellent '80s jumpsuit you lent to a so-called friend, never to be returned. You will feel so happy you had it. You will be so mad it's gone. You will be even madder that other people don't get how absolutely incomprehensible the fact that it's gone is. You'll be lonelier than you've ever been yet feel more understood when you're standing amongst the people that get it. You'll feel So Much Guilt. It's really tiring – having that fired at you 24/7. But if you know this and you can get more comfortable with its chaotic nature, it might be marginally less terrible. Let's have a little look at a few of the emotions you're likely to come across. Some of which Emma has already mentioned but bear repeating because they're the biggies and some that are more likely to pop up if you're an extrovert. Or just really like shouting.

Sadness I don't have to walk you through the sadness because you got that. You feel it. It's in your bones. Boringly predictable. You will feel like you are both a very wet duvet and the mid-section of Sinead O'Connor's "Nothing Compares 2U". You can go through sadness with ease, whether you're like me and want to plaster it on a 140ft bill board in Piccadilly Circus[2] or you're like Emma and want to hold it very close and very tight, turning it over and over in your hands until it's worn smooth.

Guilt The one you've all come for. Man, oh man. Will you feel some guilt. Uncharacteristically, I agree with Emma here, I reckon guilt is the mind's way of tricking you into not looking at the sad. It's self-preservation. Make it all about how bad you were, focus in on it and you sneakily bypass the feelings that make your throat close up. And it lingers there so you just keep replaying scenes trying to change the ending. You know that ending can't be changed but your mind just gave you a job and it probably did it to stop you completely falling apart. I have felt so much guilt. Guilt about letting friendships slip away or shouting at people until they were unsustainable. Guilt about losing very precious things: I still, on a monthly basis, wonder if I should get a metal detector to try to find my Nan's tiger's eye ring she lent me and I lost. When I was four. I feel guilt about the years of not speaking to my Mum that I won't get back even though they have been the most peaceful of my life. But bereavement guilt is

---

1 Or Times Square for our international audiences – Bonjour, Zdravstvuyte, Konnichiwa!

something else. I regretted everything. Not getting married before she died. Not getting to the hospice sooner. Not being nicer. Ruining her last Christmas. Yep, that is a toughie. Because my Nan and I were very close and very similar and she systematically hid the fact she was going to die from us all, we had a massive row on her final Christmas. I acted like any stupid ass in their twenties would with a parent they figured was immortal. And then she wasn't and I had ruined the last of her favourite days. It is physically painful to write that BUT now it is not all I think about all of the time. I can accept that I am just one of the many members of the family that have ruined Christmas over the years. I can acknowledge that I am not even the only person that pissed her off that day.[3] I can look at our dynamic and think "not ideal but at least we were truly us". You'll probably have an equivalent guilt and you'll probably hold it for the rest of your life. Just take a breath every time you do, hold it at arm's length, examine all its nooks and crannies and then position it on your memory shelf nestled amongst everything else. It won't seem so unforgivable then, I'm sure.

Fear OK, so I've touched on this – the double whammy is coming up. Let's get the worst one out the way first. If you're here because you watched someone die it was probably very frightening. On a primal level. You now know what's coming for you. You see how very fragile we are and how unlike the cinematic version of people dying it is. It will play back in your mind and you will feel horrified. Go. To. A. Therapist. They will help you reframe it. As a culture we've

---

3 A family friend turned up, unannounced, and invited himself for dinner, making a disastrous 13 people round the table, so I had to eat in the back room alone because superstition dictates the world was going to end if someone didn't sacrifice themselves. Ironically, the world ended anyway.

OSS
L SS
LO S
LOS
LOSS

categorically failed to prep anyone for this element of loss and it's a stinker. There seems to be a similar reticence in talking about birth but there are no NCT classes to prepare you for watching someone die. More's the pity. Then there's the fear of yourself and for yourself. Just so much stuff. Conversely, if you lost someone or something precious and you weren't there at the crucial point of no return there's also the fear of what it might have been like. You'll be scared you could have made it easier, more peaceful or project managed it so it would sit in your mind palace more comfortably than the huge glaring void of infinite shit possibilities you have now. You are essentially damned if you do and damned if you don't. Either way, you'll likely be so sad and so angry and so all over the place that you'll feel you have no handle on anything. You might feel this way forever and then what would be the point? It is the very worst kind of torture. Just take one breath at a time when it's all a haze. Make no big decisions. Perhaps write everything down in a big book of things to look at next month/year/decade. Let yourself be scared because this is terrifying. But also look outwards and know that other people made it back from the precipice. You will too.

And if you're here for a different kind of loss and it frightened you, then you are well within your rights to say that too. Anything that pulls the rug out from under you is frightening because the thing about the rug being pulled is that the first and most pressing matter you focus on is the fall. You are plummeting downwards, you don't know how and where you're going to land and there's a good chance it's going to really hurt. No-one has to have died for you to feel scared of that – it's innate and natural and you're absolutely valid in feeling that way so don't feel weird about expressing it.

Happiness It's a bit like sadness. Revel in it. If you're sad that you have lost a thing, then that is because the thing was astonishing and unique and utterly wonderful. Take yourself down memory lane. Those little vignettes aren't going anywhere and, again, our minds seem to go into autopilot and set them in technicolour. I know the details will fade away and that will be really hard to bear but the big screen version of the person/place/thing you lost can honestly be such a salve. Bathe in those moments. I like to get out the photo albums and make my family look at them as often as I can. It makes my Nan into a fairytale. Something they can get lost in and take so much joy from. Yes, there will be pain that the story ended where it did, when there were so many adventures left to have, but what a glorious stroke of luck we had her in the first place – the very best of women. Same with the old colleagues you've accumulated from jobs you miss, the blurry scenes of your childhood before a parent left, the insane chemistry you had with a partner 20 years ago, uni friends who remember all the reckless jollity now slipped away, including the explosion of colour you all were in your youth. Anything that's gone is still there, in a way, otherwise it wouldn't be such a wrench to lose it. But let's flip reverse it. What if you haven't got very happy memories of the lost thing? You might, I know it sounds awful, feel happy that someone or something that caused you pain and torment has gone. That is OK too. Again, I would advise getting some therapy pronto, 'cos that is an emotional tangle of epic proportions, but it is perfectly understandable to feel a joy at being released from an unbearable situation and to have those invisible bonds of trauma snipped. You probably aren't happy they're gone, you're happy that you're free. The loss you're experiencing might be you mourning for the life you could have had if that element hadn't been present. Completely understandable. If you take only one thing from this book, I hope it's that whatever you feel is perfectly natural and as complex and uniquely yours as your own fingerprint. The only thing to keep tabs on is whether it's manifesting in a safe and nourishing way.

Anger I spent a lot of the first few years after Nan died being really mad. At family and friends for not being supportive enough or, not congratulating me on doing so well despite my hideous loss and coddling me. I was mad Nan had died. I was mad other people who weren't as wonderful as she was hadn't died. I was mad the world was just going on like it hadn't happened. I was mad my life was on hold and the world seemed to have stopped. I was mad no one understood me. I was mad when people said they understood me because how could they possibly understand this MISERY. I think you can see where this is going. I was just very, very cross. And I told people. Far too directly. If you're like Emma you probably won't tell people but resolve to secretly and eternally hate them. Whatever your predicament and however you deal, anger is likely to be up there with some of your more frequent, uncontrollable and completely baffling feelings. It's annoying and also a quick route back to guilt. Which is nice.

So you've got your sadness, your fear, your guilt, your happiness, your anger (and all the sub-emotions: despair, optimism, pessimism, ennui, the unrelenting need to control, etc.) and they all feed into how you react to everything. Again, uniquely based on you. Again, often highly predictable. Think of it like Monica from *Friends* explaining the erogenous zones to Chandler. It's like that. We just hit our preferred ones in our own singular, subconscious order. Unfailingly, my emotions make me do this in times of trouble:

1. Get mad (anger)
2. Freak out (fear)
3. Distract myself and try to change something (control)
4. Fall on the floor crying (sadness)

You can apply that to any experience of loss for me.

I have lost my trainers = get mad at my husband, Jamie, for putting them somewhere. Freak out I'll never be able to replace them. Distract myself and indulge my need to control the situation – meaning relentlessly looking for replacements on eBay and finally fall on the floor crying.

I have lost my job = get mad at the company/circumstances for creating a situation in which I have to leave the job. Freak out I'll never be able get another job. Distract myself and indulge my need to control the situation by plotting the downfall of bad bosses/the world or looking for another job and finally fall on the floor crying.

I have lost a friendship = get mad at the person I've grown apart from for not being better very specifically in the context of my life. Freak out I'll never be able get that friend back (even though we've clearly grown apart). Distract myself and indulge my need to control by trying to make the best of it and reframe a relationship that's very much run its course and finally fall on the floor crying.

Embarrassingly predictable. Sometimes OK, sometimes wildly unhealthy. Particularly if you're someone who really goes deep on the need to control a situation as there the path to madness lies. And there are so many ways to do it. Trying to control your psychological thermostat by conducting some high-risk emotional and sexual behaviour? Therapist. Trying to control your reduced ability to self-soothe by medicating yourself into feeling OK? Therapist. Trying to control your body and contort it to the kind of diminished shape that reflects every facet of your self being left utterly wanting? Therapist. Want to corral your family into acting like the Waltons so you feel like it's All Going To Be Fine? Ther. A. Pist.

The wild cards

Expanding on my very succinct examples above, there will actually be myriad ways the emotions squeeze themselves out of you, and the accompanying behaviours can be really bloody challenging. For you and all the people around you. Which is an instant "Go To Guilt Jail" card. Sorry. Do Not Pass Go and Do Not Collect £200. They're cyclical and they'll be old crutches that manifest in new ways, masquerading as helpful but in actual fact they're probably doing absolutely nothing for your posture. In bereavement, I really doubled down on mine. They were enhanced enough to scare the shit out of people but because they weren't instantly life-threatening, no-one really mentioned them. You might be doing this too, so be really honest with yourself, have a ponder on what your more caustic coping strategies are and whether you're practicing them right now. Spoiler: you almost certainly are.

Mine are painfully predictable, the first of which is to stop eating. And weigh myself. Every day. It's my go-to and has been since my early teens. But I ramped it up with goals and mania and only eating certain percentages of food on my plate. I romanticized it. I felt that the nearly one stone that dropped from my pretty thin body was a perfectly normal response to the single most nourishing person in my life being gone. I honestly thought a little bit of my soul had detached and floated away like that film *21 Grams*. My Nan was in all ways a feast and now I just had a table of dust in front of me. I counted my ribs and thought it was all completely marvellous and dramatic and natural. Except it was as unnatural as me eating half a slice of toast and an egg a day. I also threw the dial up on my "straight-talking, no-nonsense Northern persona." This is one I see a lot. Hurt people, hurt people, to coin a gross saying. I absolutely hated so many perfectly supportive and reasonable friends and told a fair few so. I told them off for not asking enough or resolved to put them out my life. I told people off for caring about other stuff too. I was cruel. And selfish. To provoke people was one of the only ways I could feel in a pronounced way. I shared too much and listened too little. I got to the point I would have a panic attack if I was talking in front of more than four or five people. I became so anxious about my health I lived as though I was dying every day. Because the thing about losing someone is that often, the way that you lost them will be the way you dread losing anyone who doesn't answer your call on the second ring.

So yes, the resulting behaviours are awful and tiring and you might well be a drag, BUT the people that matter will stick with you, deflecting emotional missiles like the fucking

SAS and waiting for you to get back to some semblance of normality. You will get there. You can't feel guilty about not being there yet, but it's probably good to look at how you're affecting other people. And that's coming from someone who rarely, if ever, thinks about how they're affecting other people. Maybe set a calendar reminder as an active way to examine things.[4] Just look outwards once in a while, as impossible as that might seem. It'll provide a handy break for your frazzled mind. Don't go too far the other way though. It's very easy, if you're an introvert, to jam all the emotions into the emotional lockbox for fear of being a terrible burden. It's OK to be a bit of a burden, people can take your weight.

In summary, experiencing loss is just throwing into relief all the things we feel every day and then adding some more rogue emotions for good measure. Then they get mixed up (like Rachel's trifle in *Friends*). It tastes like crap to most people but crucially it will not kill you. It's just mince and cream. It's going to take a lot to force it down and you are probably going to have quite the upset stomach (literally, emotions do some funky shit to your body) but crucially, you will survive it and be armed with a much better understanding of how to navigate the various terrible layers of it next time. *Bon appétit.*

---

4 Like my husband does to remind him to tell me he loves me. We're a very aspirational couple.

ACTION STATIONS
How to channel all those feelings the right way.

- Elect a friend to be your voice of reason. If you worry you're being wayward, task that pal with pulling you up when you're being a twat. They have to be a close friend and you have to commit to not getting offended. It's a tough balance but if you get it right, it's gold.

- Write things down. If you get something down on paper, very often it won't seem as abjectly terrible as it is in your mind, so this is good for diffusing thoughts that are mushrooming.

- Make an accountability alarm. Set a once-a-week reminder to think about the things you put into the world. This is good for getting you out of your own head for a minute and keeps you connected to your empathy dial. This doesn't need any actions, but if you feel like you've been an arse, just try to be kinder next week.

Dr Sheetal Says...

The result of loss is generally not only that the thing or person is suddenly missing from your life, but also that it can dredge up old insecurities and memories as well as bringing about new complications. This can be overwhelming and lead to wanting to stem those feelings or – as we therapists say a lot – AVOID. Avoidance is such a brutal word, but we do essentially do just that when we don't want to experience the pain that doing, seeing or feeling something might cause. Makes sense, right? Why on earth would we throw ourselves into the boxing ring of pain and allow ourselves to be knocked out in round two. It's both humiliating and painful. But sometimes therapy is a bit like stepping into the ring and giving as well as receiving blows in equal measures for many rounds until you finally prevail and are able to knock down that thing you're afraid of.

"Almost loss", the idea that someone *could* have left (or died), or that something was almost lost, may leave you traumatized and fearful of this happening again, because you almost witnessed it and it was bloody terrifying. I have seen that the effects of this can be as haunting as loss itself and can lead to symptoms of post-traumatic stress disorder (PTSD). Worrying about something that hasn't happened lends itself to believing fear is helpful. Unfortunately a loss would result in a challenging time anyway and no amount of worry will reduce the impact when it comes. Sometimes we become so used to feeling a certain way that it almost becomes comfortable even if it is as terrifying as fear. Somehow stepping out of that comfort zone feels scarier than the prospect of trying to make yourself feel better. Notice the patterns that allow the avoidance to occur and practise taking the armour away in short doses. Practise feeling vulnerable.

"

I put on my bra, insert the left breast,

size two, tear-shape

and think of you kissing that space,

closer to my heart's rhythm than
anyone before

and to the things that change it.
"

"I found my lump on the night Princess Diana died. Three weeks later she was drowned under a tidal wave of cellophane and flowers, and I had only one breast. Always a 34A, I thought it wouldn't matter much, but it did. There's often a kind of shame associated with loss. I felt it as a child when my father died; I felt the same about my mastectomy – not wanting anyone to see the scar. But 24 years later I'm still glad I decided against reconstruction – my small perky breast with its one freckle could never have been re-constructed: a (probably male) cosmetic surgeon would have constructed something quite other; my flat bony chest and its silvery scar belong entirely to me. I'm lucky to live in the age of the stick-on silicone prosthesis I can put on in the morning, peel off at night and more or less forget about. But there is joy in putting the flat of my hand against my ribs, feeling my heart still beating, able to remember wearing '70s dresses with no bra, sunbathing naked, and my son feeding, on his favourite side."

Poet and lecturer Alicia Stubbersfield on the loss of her breast, that saved her life. Written in response to her poem *The Doctor Makes a Suggestion*.

LOSS CLUB

When you're going through a loss, do you need to share it or keep it to yourself? Either way, here's how to make use of the people around you to help you get through it.

Emma: Sometimes, through loss you find yourself in weird situations with people you don't know that well. Sometimes your loss community is not your existing community.

Robyn: Yes, I think the breadth and depth of people who've lost something big is incredible and can help you put this mystifying thing into context.

Emma: It's amazing how you come across additional members of your loss squad along the way.

Robyn: Totally, you grow a sonar for broken people. An SOS beacon, and it operates silently, and you find people that you just think are great people, but they're also making the little whale song. And then you get hammered and it turns out everyone has a dead parent, and so you unconsciously collect the people you need.

ROBYN ON LOSS CLUB

Musings from the one who needs do it as part
of a collective

There is nothing more validating than someone saying "I know exactly what you mean" and it being true. It's a long exhale when you feel like you've been holding your breath for months. It's euphoria and relief. It's everything.

Despite being desperate to be part of any gang going, I have always felt like an outsider. Probably because the most lauded (and sometimes most damaging) of all human relationships was not available to me. That unbreakable mother–daughter bond? Not there. The warming glow of her pride and unerring adoration, ribboning through my marrow, allowing me to face any challenge life threw at me? Not a bit of it. I never felt loved by the one person who society tells you is biologically programmed to do so. In fact, a good portion of the time I felt like she actively hated me. Because she told me so. Peak melodrama, hey? But it's true. I was not part of the world's easiest-to-join club: membership 7,799,999,996[1]. As a result I've always felt a bit fundamentally unnatural and at a distance from other people while simultaneously needing them to a completely unreasonable degree. I'm the friend you always hoped for. Not.

That meant I got acquainted with loss real early as I pined for a relationship I'd never really had but felt that I knew intimately and needed all-consumingly because I saw it. EVERYWHERE. It also meant that whenever I was presented with any sense of commonality it gave my

---

1 That's the world population minus me, Matilda from Roald Dahl's *Matilda* and the little boy from *Goodnight Mr Tom*. All other people's mum's love them. It's on the group flag and in the motto.

a long exhale

a long exhale

a long exhale

a long exhale

a long exhale

a long exhale

a long exhale

a long exhale

a long exhale

a long exhale

a long exhale

a long exhale

a long exhale

a long exhale

drum-tight nerves a moment to soften, and my heart would grow three sizes. Because as George Orwell says: "Perhaps one did not want to be loved so much as to be understood."

As I grew up in such an extraordinarily chaotic – and, often traumatic – way, to experience recognition felt like a benediction. Never was this more true than in times of loss, when I have felt so unknowable and so very, very alone. I can't begin to express my gratitude to the other little lost souls that spoke to me, sometimes wordlessly, when I needed them most. And I can confidently say without being a complete psychopath "and vice versa." From schoolfriends who had a similarly "alternative" family set-up and I knew judged nothing, to colleagues who had also lost a loved one and whose almost imperceptible tenderness carried me through. The pals who also pushed away a parent because they had to and made it feel like it wasn't a filthy secret. A disproportionate number of teachers who scooped up a motherless little girl in a way that I now know was because they too probably felt unmothered. The ones who mourned turning their backs on industries too toxic, ended relationships too damaging or lost irreplaceable things. Without you all it would have been completely insurmountable. Life, I mean. So I am ALL about emotional clubs, with or without a uniform. But preferably with a uniform. Black. With an enormous veil, ideally.

The OGs

My family were my original loss club as we talked all the time. About not much and everything all at once. We're natural orators. And part of that is relaying heart-breaking moments as brush-off asides. That after Auntie Eve's fiancé died in the war she chose not to have another relationship because you "never love like that again". That it's collectively acknowledged that my Nanny Al willed her broken heart to putter out when she lost her soulmate. We share because it's a weird communal therapy and a way of working through something indirectly. We don't like lots of emotional effort and we do like a show-stopping party anecdote so it's double-bubble.

As soap opera-ish and infuriating as my family can be, they are mine and I know them completely. They are the club that I've most felt a part of, even when I've been desperate to leave. It's not always been the best club. In fact, it's sometimes felt like a damaging cult or a multi-level marketing conference with everyone shouting their messaging Very Bloody Loud, but they are a piece of me and I love them, even the ones I don't see.

HOWEVER, when it came to the great Barbara Bereavement of 2009, they were next to useless. As a support network they were actively unhelpful. I think, annoyingly, families can be the absolute worst people to turn to when you experience a big communal loss because everyone goes into their own heads while, simultaneously, letting their expectations for others skyrocket. I wanted to be enveloped in the comforting bosom of my Nan's family. What I got was shouting, public discord, an estrangement, an embarrassing funeral snubbing, feeling at the time that my grandad moved on a little too quickly, my dad forgetting to ask if I was OK then fucking off to Norway and all of us feeling quite cross that we weren't being understood or considered.

The chances are you're too close to your family to gauge how effective an emotional buoy they realistically are when broken down into their component parts (mine were a single water wing, a loudhailer and a flask of tea that I was directed to make myself) and not close enough to be able to articulate what you want and what you can offer in return. It's eggshell city and someone stole your shoes.[2] That's OK. Just take a breath. One top tip is to grab a metaphorical or actual notepad. Look at your family as if you were David Attenborough examining a very tiny chameleon. Quietly and at a safe distance. Note down what kind of animal they are. Their habits. Their nature. Then look at that list and be realistic about what they can offer you. The fact you share DNA doesn't come into this. Maybe they can offer nothing at all. That's OK. You can look elsewhere.

Unconscious outsourcing

I believe one thing very firmly. That my heart gives off a sonar. And it talks to other hearts and guides them to me when I'm in an SOS situation. It has always happened. The people I need turn up at the right moment and in an unspoken way I know we are the same. Mainly because you seem to develop a very dark sense of humour when you're well acquainted with loss. You will draw people to you that just seem great generally and then one drunken night they'll turn to you and mumble "When my mum died..." or "Yes, I too have known abuse," or "I feel I don't even know who I am anymore" or anything really. And you'll go "YES, ME TOO. I knew there was a reason why I liked you." Those people are worth their weight in gold. The ones you wordlessly call to you. It can be macro.

---

2   This is a perfect example of family storytelling. My Uncle Jimmy has a reputation for grabbing people's shoes in hotels and moving them to different floors. For larks. Uncle Jimmy is as Uncle Jimmy does. He also wore sunglasses to my Nana's funeral. Like Arnie in *The Terminator*.

Remark on a woman's lovely hair at a friend's birthday party and then find yourself crying on the South Bank at 3am because bullying bosses *did* make a career in fashion impossible for both of you and that really is bloody unfair. Or it can be two people talking about the insurmountable loss of a child or a spouse, or the opportunity to live to the ripe old age they were expecting, or any of the massive things people have to deal with. Whatever loss you're carrying around, that secret club is so utterly validating and precious and essential. It's like finding the other mad scientist doing their research on the mating habits of the rainbow-bearded thornbill hummingbird and being able to feverishly whack out your notes and compare them. In the white lab coats you're inevitably sporting, stained with tears.

For me, these people are the core members of Loss Club. They have read the manual cover to cover. They have performed the Myers–Briggs test on you and established you're a complementary personality type and, most importantly, they want to be there. You'll love them for who they are and what they represent. I reminisce on them all with a mixture of profound gratitude, a weird fraternal love and ongoing amusement, because they were always a ride. That's my love language – bad jokes and big-time sharing. And gifts. Which they all were.

These happened-upon companions can be transformative but remember they are based on a mutual open-door policy. If you put your sad in the box and close the lid then no one can hear the sonar and so people who might be a comfort just cruise on by. It would be such a shame to miss them so try to stay open to the possibility of camaraderie in those lonely times, someone might just nudge the door and surprise you.

The classified ads of ennui

There are lots, and I mean LOTS of actual, formalized clubs out there dealing with every type of loss you can imagine. You can go and find a group of people who are dealing with the exact trauma you are experiencing, and you can sit with them and you can discuss it and there will probably be sandwiches. I imagine it can be super rewarding. If you're that way out then fill your boots (but not in a Marla Singer way). I confess, perhaps surprisingly, that I've never done one. But that's probably because I don't like public speaking or a good chunk of the populous. Based on no experience whatsoever, I have surmised that you are going to get some showboating assholes in that kind of group discussion situation and in times of upheaval my patience for people like that is almost non-existent. I can be very rude (and I suspect am one of those showboating assholes). Either way it didn't appeal to me, but it could work for you so think about it, huh. A very, very much more low-impact way of dipping your toe into actual support groups is by doing it digitally. It's how Emma and I found our wider community. We came up with Other's Day on Instagram (see page 296) after making a few throw-away statements about how the marketing around Mother's Day was a bit relentless and bummed us out. And then hundreds of people slid into our DMs and said "Yeah, same." So we decided to just carve out a little space on the internet for people who felt sad too, so they could express that rather than sulk in a corner about the fact that "No, a Mother-Daughter crafting box was not just the thing for this time of year." At least not for them. And it opened our eyes to all the people who felt discombobulated on those kind of days for a thousand different reasons: from miscarriage to estrangement to slowly losing a parent to dementia to, well, just to the power of infinity. All these people had lost something and just wanted to simply be able to say that without being made to feel like a party pooper, and in a space where someone else might be able to empathize and make them feel a little less Terribly Alone. Fast-forward a few years and we've been on the telly (nice), we've spoken to loads of lovely Other's Day cohorts (really nice) and some brands have tried to co-opt it for commercial gain (less nice). And that's just in our minuscule corner of the internet.

To really drive home my point about the power of digital gaggles, just think of mothers. They are the perfect example of the power of the internet and of loss clubs. Early motherhood sounds a lot like early bereavement. You are most likely sleep-deprived, confused, scared, doing something no one prepared you for, everyone else seems to be having a much better time than you, no one seems to have noticed you're literally falling apart and you wish you could fashion yourself a time machine because this situation could not be borne in any meaningful long-term way. Enter the Instamum. There will be one you connect to whether they're doing send-up ditties about how much they currently dislike their baby. Or publicly crying 'cos it's all too much. Or posting a photo of themselves smeared in faeces, asking for advice on mastitis or just saying they haven't a clue what's going on. And while they work through this confusing new world there are thousands of people conversing with them saying "I got you" or "cabbage leaves" or "Vanish is really good at getting shit out." And in that way navigating their new normal is a little less completely unbearable because everyone feels they have someone who gets it. Or so I'm told.

I'm also told that for some people, and I'm sure not the majority (because if it was why would anyone procreate?), but for *some* people, the moment you become a mother it's quite normal to feel loss in a way you couldn't even have imagined: a loss of yourself, of your girlhood, of your freedom. That you mourn yourself and the woman you were and while you wouldn't take it back for a moment, something is lost that will never return. We need to make a space to talk about that properly, because it sounds pretty intense.

Complementary therapy

Then we come to the people who haven't had your type of loss, who don't get it, but who can be a really nice weapon in your uplifting arsenal regardless. They are the sidenotes. The welcome distractions. The little slivers of normality in a world that feels foreign. There will still be some touchpoints on familiarity, but their otherness will be a joy and you'll almost certainly funnel in a good helping of loss. That's all very abstract but I'll give you a concrete scenario based on me (because I love to talk about me).

I embarked on a Creative Writing MA two months after my Nan died. It was poor timing. But it was also excellent timing. I got to spend time with people who I had something in common with, i.e. creatives, who were not grieving and were not related to me, and I got to write stuff down. That was really liberating. And I got to channel all my sadness into starting a novel that was a thinly veiled autobiographical look at loss and otherness[3]. I did that alongside 14 other people all repackaging their stuff and creating some terrible and some jolly good literature as a result. I sat firmly in the

---

3 Except in it I was a young, male homosexual traveller with a passion for millinery.

middle. I was passable. But those people, and three in particular who also felt a bit other but didn't directly get my experience, were a godsend. They gave me somewhere to be once a week. Gave me somewhere to put my sadness. Gave me somewhere to get away from it too. Those classmates are and were awesome, even the ones who were just there for comic effect. The distractions. The people who reminded me that you could focus in on really annoying, insignificant things and that was OK. They gave me bad poetry and really good vibes. They made me want to be cleverer and more well read and less of a drag. One carried me home when I was so drunk I couldn't physically lift my face off the table after a particularly ropey open mic night. One dropped me on the floor from such a great height that I regularly flash back to the hideous tipping point. One asked me the most direct and disarming questions I've ever been asked and made me chauffeur him round like he was Lady Penelope. They made me know what it would be to feel normal again. And they were very gentle with my sometimes achingly shit writing. I'll touch on them again later in the book, but the point is that sometimes it's really helpful to find a loss group that isn't about loss, whether that's a pottery class or beginners' Italian or samba. Trust that the people in it will be good people, because they share a passion with you and will probably offer some respite from the relentless monotony of working through your grief.

And that's Loss Club. The secret is really the whole world is Loss Club but I've just done you a Time Out *Places to Find Companionship in a Time of Loss* article to take all the stress out of trying to muddle it out. Think of me as an emotional concierge. You're welcome.

ACTION STATIONS
Getting the club dynamic right.

- Make an unspoken time limit for sharing in the Loss Club sharing circle. To get Loss Club business off your chest can feel wonderful but you might drown out the Emmas in your life. Keep the time you're taking up the mic in your mind because listening is as precious as speaking.

- Members don't have to be for life. You might not feel as comfortable sharing a current loss with a historic friend. Just because they're an old familiar doesn't mean they're the right man for the job. You aren't obliged to confide. Trust your gut.

- Don't get fixated on fixing things. Loss Club is primarily about sharing. You can't just bulldoze in and try and save the day. Sometimes being inert is the most dynamic thing you can do.

EMMA ON LOSS CLUB
Musings from the one who tried to do it all by herself

Here I am, back in the studio, because there are no people in the studio and that's how I like it, how I tried to do loss and how I low-key think my best life would be. Does that sound about as far away from Loss Club as it's possible to be? Probably. I think whenever I'm writing you might find it helpful to think of me as a hermit in the woods who doesn't like clubs.

But if only Loss Club *were* a real club. A place full of everybody who knows and loves you, where you can go and be enveloped by exactly what you need, when you need it. Feel loved and cherished, have space, be given free rein in the Smashing Room with the fine china and baseball bats. In Ideal Land, Loss Club is where everybody would go after every loss. A retreat for the bereft. Only, if Loss Club were a real club, it would probably be disappointing. Because loss is unique, you are unique, and your response to the losing of a thing will require totally different support to, say, mine. Robyn and my losses were similar in shape and scale, but what we needed in the aftermath couldn't have been more different, which meant the support we wanted from those around us was wildly different too.

This chapter's all about the universality of loss, and the community and opportunity for connection therein – the people and places where you might find support. But the truth is, I've often felt like I went through my big loss alone. Not because I was physically on my own and not because I don't have caring people in my life, but because I thought I had to. I thought that if anybody saw the real emotional response I was having they would run away screaming, so I built walls and put up big signs that said, "NO TRESPASSING

ON MY EMOTIONS", and most people stuck to the rules. And I was a little bit grateful for that, but also a little bit hurt and angry, because why didn't anybody want to scale my emotional buttresses to get in? Oh, loss, you complicated bastard. So I soldiered on and got myself in what's medically known as a right tangle, before finally finding the community I needed. It was a community of one. It was me. I found ways of getting to grips with my loss while still remaining an island. And – spoiler alert – like every odd couple film ever, once I'd done that, my little community grew, to include first Robyn a little bit, then my therapist, then Robyn even more, and my partner, Matt, then, backed up by that little crew, I was on firm enough ground to open up to other friends when I wanted to, talk openly about loss on Instagram and our blog, All Up In My Space, and – ultimately – it landed me here, writing a little book about loss to try and help other people, even those who think they have to go through it alone. Because you might want to – you might do all your best thinking and healing by yourself, and that's OK. But there are ways to give yourself a nicer time doing it, and, while you might never be the kind of person who wants to join a grief group or do improv about Covid, there are ways to build yourself your own Loss Club, even if it only has you and one or two other people in it – it still very much counts.

Hermits (don't) do it better

When loss hits, you might feel like the inside of a grilled cheese sandwich – mushy and gooey and falling apart without your usual crisp, toastie exterior. Maybe you feel like you're made of stone, or full of popping candy, or angry juice, but often once you get past those bits you're left with a gooey cheese of emotions – the raclette of sadness – that you'll need to deal with. And, as we found out in Chapter Three, when loss hits, it's likely that some less-than-optimum mental health moments might come your way. So knowing how and where to find a bit of help is going to be at least helpful, and possibly even life-changing. Dramatic? Yes, but entirely possible.

Some people will want to tell you how to do loss. Talk more! Talk less! Go on holiday! Get on with it! Get a dog! Don't get a dog! Borrow my dog! Join a group! Go on a retreat! Make jam! Paint! Make jam-paint! And they mean well and they love you and are only trying to help, but only you ever really know what you need. And sometimes you don't know what you need but you do know that doing watercolours with Liza is going to make you want to insert a paintbrush very painfully into your eye. And that's OK. What works for one person might not work for you. And what works for you, for one loss, might not work for another. When you lose the stability that a once-loved career has given you, contact with people who've also been through it might feel reassuring. But when you lose the partner you've loved for a lifetime, you might need to stay very quiet by yourself for a while and wait for your toasted sandwich to crisp up and stop your gooey insides falling out on the floor. Personally, I guard my emotional sandwich like a cartoon Doberman. It's a control thing. No shade to my parents, but lots of change in one's early years often means that we find our control wherever we can. For me, having an inside world that nobody else could touch became sacred and I'd batten down the hatches any time anybody tried to get in. That might sound familiar – trying to keep all your important bits on the inside, while from the outside you look FINE. Everything moving along nicely, nothing to see here.

Only, that means that when the insides do turn to goo, nobody knows. On the outside you might still seem fine, and people will then behave accordingly. At least, that's what happened to me.

I think people can be very uncomfortable around loss – not wanting to upset you by talking about it, but not wanting to gloss over it either – so the chances are that they'll look to you for a heads-up on how to behave, and when they see you being Totally Fine, they're likely to adopt that stance as well. And you might need to go through some of it without your nearest and dearest – that's no problemo. So long as you're finding ways to process and work through it in your way, you're doing good. In my case, there was very little focus on what was happening and very little processing going on. OK, there was zero processing going on. I spent a lot of time worrying I wasn't doing it right, was rejecting help, should be doing other things. I thought I needed to prove I was OK, but also needed to be sadder around people – needed to showcase the public grief that people expected. I drove myself a bit mad wondering why I wasn't feeling better, ever. And came to the conclusion that it was just always going to be shit. If you're at that stage now, I'm here to tell you that it isn't if you don't want it to be. Whatever you're going through – whatever you lost, whatever stage of it you're at – there are people and places you can go to, to get help. Even if you hate people and places, there are metaphorical planes you can take yourself to help get through it. Right now it might seem like the world has ended, and if you're like me, without action, it might secretly feel like that for many years. But ultimately, you will get through this loss. You'll work at it, and learn about it, and from it you'll come out a new version of yourself. I did not go through my Big

Loss in a particularly healthy way. There's so much I would change about it in hindsight, but changing things that have happened in the past isn't a skill I have, so instead I'm changing how I look at it all.

If you're hermetically-inclined, like I am, you might find it hard to open up to people about how you're feeling. And if you're as inexperienced at opening up as I was (am – I'm still learning) you might find some of the moments you do it uncomfortable or even embarrassing. For a long time the only time I'd talk to my friends about my Mum was after very many glasses of wine. I'd get drunk, cry, and wake up puffy-eyed the next day, feeling embarrassed at how emotional I'd been. You know, loss is messy like that. What I probably could've done instead of meeting friends for drinks is give myself time alone to be sad and feel those emotions. Because, in case the rest of the book wasn't making it abundantly clear: I'm the introvert. I'm the one who needs all the time and space to rest and recharge. I still struggle to cry in front of people about the big things, so if I do cry, it's often big and messy and by myself. I don't even think I cried at my Mum's funeral. Or when her hearse followed us off the ferry the next day and drove along miles of winding roads in front of us. My Mum barely even cried in front of me through it all. I think in matters involving somebody else's health we often take the lead from them on how to handle the emotional side of things. See how it's infectious? How many parents living through Covid had to check their own emotional displays to make sure the kids didn't freak out? How many friends have tiptoed around another friend's breakup for fear of setting them off? Sometimes I think we're all just waiting to be shown the right way to deal with loss.

Loss Crew, don't assemble!

Even within a loss, there are sub-losses that have to be dealt with. When a loved one dies, we often have to give away their possessions. When you lose a job, you also lose a set of friends and colleagues. When you have a big life change – even a positive one – you might feel you've lost who you used to be. A friendship lost will come with countless moments you want to tell that person about a thing and can't. An estrangement might close off certain favourite places to you. The point is, whatever you lose, it's likely you'll need support through more than just one thing. My own Big Loss was littered with other losses. An estrangement, loss of possessions, financial losses, and the loss of a last chance to say goodbye that I was never allowed when the great secret ash-scattering happened without me knowing. And because I am an introvert at a fairly extreme end of the scale, I held all those things inside to deal with by myself. It might be that that feels a bit mad to you, if you're, say, a 4.3 on the introvert scale to my 9.6. Or maybe just some of what I'm saying rings true, and that's fully OK. This book's a bit of a pick n' mix situation – you get to see which bits sound right to you and then use those to help. If you find yourself shouting, "YES!" at a particular bit, you could mark a little note next to it and, collectively at the end, that might help you to work out how much of a Robyn-esque extrovert or Emma-esque introvert you are.

As we're talking about community through loss, I'd like to throw in this note: not everybody will get it. In fact, some people might be a little bit rubbish. There, I said it. While you're busy feeling bruised like a peach in a gym bag, some people will not respond in the way you need them to.

When you have
a big life change
you might feel
you've lost who
you used to be.

When you have
a big life change
you might feel
you've lost who
you used to be.

Some people might even use your peach state for unkind ends. My top tip? Recognize those people and try making a note to not let them distract you from what you need. It might seem really tempting to go feel bad about something else for a while – like you deserve it, even, but it's only serving to distract you from helping yourself feel better, and, really, isn't that the ultimate goal?

Help yo' self

One of the only things that *both* Robyn and I did with our loss (eventually) is get therapy. But, true to form, in very different ways. Robyn in short, intense bursts and me in a planned-out, years-long journey that's ongoing today. I say today, because, whenever you're reading this, I'll still be in therapy, so valuable have I found it. I've been in weekly sessions for years, and it's no exaggeration to say that it saved my life, and changed it powerfully for the better. But, as an under-sharer who thinks they need to keep everything inside, I remember how daunting starting that journey was and inviting somebody to join my Loss Club. Like a lot of people, I started my own therapy because I was in crisis, which is probably not the best time to do it. You don't wait until the fire reaches the attic before you call the fire brigade, do you? But finding a therapist is still shrouded in so much mystery for so many of us, so, in a bid to help demystify and make it less scary, I'm going to talk a bit about what it's like, as an introvert, to have given myself this very valuable thing. I'm not going to talk group therapy, because, you know, sharing in public is fundamentally Not My Thing, so, for the record, this bit's about one-on-one, talking therapy, and if that sounds daunting as heck to my introvert crew, don't worry – I got you. I know first-hand how frightening it can be. This is designed to be less a shove into a therapist's chair, and more a helping hand, if and when you're ready to sit down yourself. I recognize that there's privilege in having the means and headspace to find help, and in the access to practitioners who can understand your lived experience, so these are my own feelings on it laid out for you to use however you see fit, and however matches your needs.

If you're whirling along, keeping busy and struggling to look at an emotion or trauma you know you need to look at, having a therapist can give you time in the week where you *have* to focus on yourself – it provides structure to work through that overwhelming pile of emotions. In your therapist, you get an impartial person who's in your corner, who you know gives a shit, and who'll hold you accountable when you go off at the deep end. And – for all my people-pleasers out there – because it's a business relationship, in which the therapist is a professional who's being paid, there's no need to feel like you're burdening that person. For somebody who feels like they have to deal with everything on their own, that can be invaluable.

But, as with all rewarding things, there's a bit of work to be done before you get to the good stuff. Lots of this is universal, whether you're intro- or extrovert, so feel free to share with anybody who needs it – I know I have. First, you have to find your therapist. And because there isn't a Tinder for therapists yet, you're gonna have to work at it just a little. It might be tempting to get in touch with your nearest therapy-loving friend and ask to see their one, but here's why I'm gonna encourage you not to do that. Number one: there is power in finding your own practitioner. Deciding you want to open up your loss community to include somebody else, doing the research and making first contact is all part of a journey towards taking your own mental health seriously. Number two: a therapist relationship is kind of sacred. Especially to people who struggle with sharing. There's a space in the world where they can freely talk, that's all for them, that they might've cultivated over years of hard work, so asking to see their therapist can be a bit like asking if you can step into their birthing pool. A bit invasive and not always appropriate. Finding that therapist can feel like a minefield, right? I get it. But sifting through it all and finding the right person – although a bit trial-and-error – can be one of the most rewarding parts of the system. So, if phones scare you (they scare me), to the internet with you. Lots of countries have a governing body for therapists, with websites designed to help you find the right one for you. In the UK, we have the British Association for Counselling and Psychotherapy (BACP), where you can go and browse therapists by what they do and how they do it. I used this as a first step, writing to ten different practitioners. Of those ten, around five wrote back, I spoke with two and then chose the one who didn't make me want to vomit into my own shoes. Take your time with your search. Google what the different approaches mean. Depending on your situation, you'll benefit from different kinds of therapy – lots of therapists offer different ways of working so it can be really helpful to find out how they apply their knowledge. But it's down to you. Pick the person you feel connected to, because your relationship with that person is going to be deeply, deeply personal. I'm talking here about private therapy, which I've been privileged enough to prioritise in my own life and finances, but there are places you can go to get therapy for free – check out our resources pages at the end of the book for more information.

I think there's been a general myth about therapy that you sit in an expensive leather chair for an hour a week and it'll immediately be a huge relief and you'll just start to feel better. That's how I used to think of it. But if you're like me and you've been suppressing a lot of stuff for a lot of years, it's probably the opposite. Therapy can be a slog. And it's supposed to be challenging and uncomfortable, because that's how change happens. You might be miserable sometimes. You might wonder why you started. You might want to quit. If you're like me, you might spend a lot of time in a staring-at-the-wall state where nobody's allowed to talk to you (fun). But then slowly you'll likely re-examine things and how they work. You'll change things. You'll almost certainly question your old ways of working and start to build new ones. Habits may change and damaging belief systems will hopefully be left behind. You might learn how to communicate better with other people and with yourself. Maybe create mental space to work out who you are and what you need in the world. Maybe all of the above, maybe none of it, maybe more – your journey will be 100 per cent your own, but every step, every session attended, every moment spent outside of your comfort zone learning how to let your inside world sometimes out, is a push in a healthier direction. In my world, therapy is a gift and an endurance exercise, and when I'm Prime Minister, we'll all be at it.

If you've just gone through a loss, even reading this chapter might feel overwhelming, but I'm here to tell you there is no pressure to do anything until you're ready. You're in the driving seat here. Those around you might have support to offer and opinions on what you could or should be doing, but unless you want to take the next step, don't. Because wanting to feel better is a bit of a watershed moment in any loss, where you look down at your Cornflake-strewn, week-old sweatshirt and think, "No more!" The truth is that you have to believe you can feel better after a loss, whether you went through it by yourself, with a partner, or with the rest of the world as part of a global pandemic. And, though your loved ones or your therapist will be there to pick you up when you fall over, it's you who's going to get yourself through this, because there's an as yet untapped power in you that you could find as part of this whole ordeal, and oh man, when you find it you're going to wonder how you ever missed it lurking in there. So, take your time, do a little bit of what this chapter recommends, do a lot. Do some today and then none for a month – it's all forward motion. And by the time you realize you're taking steps in the right direction, this bit you're in now will be a thing of the past.

ACTION STATIONS

How do you find community when you've built your emotional walls so high?

- If you want to talk to people, but find yourself clamming up when you try, write down what you want to say, even if it's just a few words, and take that with you to read from.

- Try saying yes when somebody offers you help with anything. No need to qualify it with, "Only if you want to." Just say yes, thank you and watch the support roll in. Once you've done it once, it'll get easier and easier.

- If you're really struggling, write down what you're feeling or needing in a letter. Then give it to somebody and let them know that you've written it because you're struggling to ask for help in person. The right people will understand, and sometimes even just writing the letter can help you understand yourself better.

Dr Sheetal Says...

You don't have to go through loss alone. I find it quite upsetting when people tell me that they don't want to be the person that brings down the mood with their sadness. Why the hell not? You're the one hurting. The least people can do is listen.

If you want emotional support from others who are going through the same thing, try a group who are actively grieving. The purpose is not to add to your emotional burden, but to feel like your emotions belong in the world and are unquestionably normal. On the other hand, people actively experiencing loss might not always be terribly helpful as they are going through their own hell and circumnavigating that before they can possibly contemplate sharing their findings with anyone else. If they haven't worked it out yet, how can they help you? Just being sad and emotional together and navigating this with someone means a burden shared, even if it doesn't immediately seem to change anything.

We are all deserving of support. Imagine if Debbie has a great, understanding support system that really gets her and gives her what she needs in terms of emotional support, space, distraction, in all the right quantities and at the right time. But Raj is isolated, has few friends and a family that don't understand. Do you think that Raj doesn't deserve the same support Debbie has? I hope not. Just because Raj was dealt a different style of support branch in life doesn't mean that he should suffer more. And that's where – for me – therapists can be invaluable. We provide support when others don't or can't. We also come in when people don't feel comfortable talking to those they know, or feel like they will be judged.

Seeking help from strangers can feel daunting, and that's normal. We know this and try to put you at ease as much as we can. We want to help, not disarm you or make you feel uncomfortable in any way. We create space where you may have struggled to and we don't rush anything.

"One of the most valuable sessions I have learned in bereavement is that grief is bespoke, different for everyone, and that a one-size-fits-all approach is sometimes unhelpful, because if your experience does not fit the pattern, you might think you are doing it wrong.

So I welcome
[conversations] about
loss – all sorts of loss –
because they help to map
a varied and unpredictable
landscape rather than
tell you what you should
be doing."

Author, musician and priest, Richard
Coles, on the unknowable nature of grief

THE WIDE WORLD

The world is full of things that have sprung from loss. From films to art and back through poetry, there are ways to use these things to help you get through your own loss.

Robyn: I find a massive comfort in knowing people can repackage loss and create something remarkable, because then it has a purpose in the world. I feel seen and less alone.

Emma: Whereas I don't want to feel seen and I want to be alone.

Robyn: Yeah, your love is a tiny, complex poem.

EMMA ON THE WIDE WORLD

An intrepid exploration of all the world has to offer a mourning introvert

I say mourning because when you lose anything, there's a period of shock, miscellaneous emotions, adjustment and reconciliation to go through. Whether you misplace a hat or your best person dies, it's all somewhere on the same spectrum and you'll do it in your own personal way. If you're somebody who likes to spend a lot of time on their own, for example, loss presents its own challenges. Because people – lovely people – will want to rally around you and Make It All Better, when what you really need is space and time to process what's happened. But then, if you're anything like me, when you're alone, maybe the emotions are difficult to get to. Maybe you organize your sock drawer into alphabetical colour order, make a papier-mâché friend for the cat and mow your neighbour's lawn instead of letting the actual feelings happen. Because the truth is that loss is complicated. You might do all the distractions, you might *want* to feel sad, but can't quite get there – if you've been boxing up what's inside your whole life, often what's in there gets all jammed up and impossible to reach. Sometimes when I'm emotionally constipated like this, Robyn will tell me to put on a playlist of sad songs and have a good old cry, and I'll look puzzled and change the subject. Because that is categorically not how I work. The idea of being able to look outside of myself to process loss or let something else influence my emotions feels alien and weird and gives me that cross feeling you get when you've just smashed your favourite mug. And likewise, Robyn finds it unfathomable that I don't want to bathe myself in the bubbling waters of music and poems and movies about loss. Because she feels seen by them. I just feel annoyed.

If you're an introvert who needs space and time to process loss alone, having loss reflected back at you through culture can feel invasive, make you angry and cause you to isolate, which means you run the risk of becoming an island. Loss Island. The saddest place in the world. But, contrary to what my inner voice has been telling me my whole life, there are ways for us introverts to take what the world has to offer and use it to help us reset and focus, access those emotions and help ourselves take another step on the long road to understanding our losses. And yes, it might seem out of character for an introvert to look outside themselves for processing tools – I was surprised to find out I even had any, but I do. Where Robyn looks for the "disgusting euphoria" of loss in culture, I'm about surrounding myself with the quiet little moments of emotional indulgence that let me drop the façade of everything being FINE, even if only for myself, and admit that sometimes I'm really not OK.

Wailing and gnashing of teeth

Some people LOVE HAVING BIG EMOTIONS. Love them. Revel in them. Want to roll around on the floor in glitter made of them. Love any movie that makes them feel things; weep uncontrollably to sad songs and flail dramatically when they read a maudlin poem. Me, not so much. I like having emotions, sure – they let me know that I'm a functioning human – but I like to have them quietly, by myself and then to think about what it all means for a bit. So, for me, anything that tries to access my emotions without my prior consent, whether that's a schmaltzy movie or a loved one, feels like an invasion, and is summarily shut down. Nobody stonewalls emotional prying quite like an introvert. You might recognise the squirmy feeling that happens when somebody starts talking about something you don't want to give away – a little bit flustered, a little bit irritated, a little bit like a stray dog backed into a corner. Those somethings are yours. They are precious. Maybe they're the only part of you that feels like it's really your own. So it stands to reason that the idea of trying to force out those emotions with something from the outside world will feel like a hideous imposition. In which case, what can introverts do with *everything in the world* through a loss? Well, it turns out, quite a lot. From art to the great outdoors and back again, we can seek out the emotional duvet that the world has to offer and swaddle ourselves in it, in micro moments that help to stop us spontaneously combusting.

I'll level with you: at the starting line of writing of this chapter I'd have said that I do not use culture to help me through loss. Nature: yes. Alone time: yes. Culture: no, no, no. But it turns out, actually, I do, just not in quite the full-immersion, grief-veil way Robyn craves. And if you don't recognize yourself in that model of grieving either, this bit's for you.

The thing about loss is that, for lots of us, it's highly personal, very private and not for anybody else's mucky hands to touch. And, as established in the previous chapter, it can be easy to believe – or even want – to go through it all alone, so to pick up a book about somebody else's great loss feels like we're not giving our own adequate attention – like that loss is competing with our own, which is largely unhelpful, and likely to make a person throw the book on the metaphorical fire. Both – and everything in between – are valid. At one end of the scale, Robyn uses art and poetry to feel seen, connected and anchored in the world, while I at the other end, use it in entirely the opposite way. It turns out I use it to spirit myself away to another place – an emotional plane that acts as a gateway to the real me. Who knew? A cursory glance around my home offers some clues as to the me I'm trying to get to. The painting of a distant lonely figure standing on the edge of a cliff, in melancholic blues and greys; the portrait of a sad horse you'd swear was about to shed a tear – the art I've chosen to hang around me is desolate. But when I look at those pictures I feel a sense of comfort; of belonging; a feeling that's peculiar only to me. And I think therein lies the nugget of gold: where some will use culture as a way to feel connected to others and reassured by the passing of similar experiences, others might use it as a secret slice of emotional pie, best enjoyed alone.

What I've learned is that while Robyn uses culture to fuel a feeling of community and connection, I use it to get in touch with myself. We really are a predictable pair. Because we introverts need to retreat to process, it's unlikely you'll find us weeping in a crowded gallery or tearing at our clothes in a Saturday matinee. What we're more likely to be doing is spending time by ourselves in nature, going for long windy walks, or being cocooned away at home in the quiet, where we can unfurl and do a bit of healing. And it's in those places – in genuine solitude – that we can find ourselves surrounded with little touchpoints that reflect our insides back at us. And, though I didn't realize it, finding those things is something I've been doing since childhood.

Be your own sad donkey

It's telling that the character I've always related to most in *Winnie the Pooh* is Eeyore. That morose donkey with self-esteem issues just speaks to my sensibilities (and is maybe why I harbour a secret desire to open a donkey sanctuary in my later years). The solitary misery, the outsider status and almost comic emotional inertia – it's classic Emma Territory. Not to mention we both have nail-on tails. This quote from *The House at Pooh Corner* pretty much perfectly sums it up. Eeyore's sad and annoyed because nobody stops around to talk to him, when Rabbit bounds on by...

> *"It's your fault, Eeyore. You've never been to see any of us. You just stay here in this one corner of the Forest waiting for the others to come to you. Why don't you go to THEM sometimes?"*

And – much as I hate to admit it, that damn rabbit is right. Sometimes it takes a children's story character to point out what you most need to see. But all stories and characters come from somewhere, and perhaps Eeyore was A. A. Milne's way of communicating some of his own darker side. That's a pretty literal example of seeing yourself reflected in culture, but I do think there's something in those characters we're introduced to as children, because my other early memory of feeling emotionally connected to culture was *Dumbo*. The misfit baby elephant separated from his mother and taught the ways of the world by a happy-go-lucky mouse. I'm gonna acknowledge here that adult me understands the shamefully racist overtones of that early Disney film, and fully condemns the dehumanization and caricaturing of black people in it. It's not a film I'd be showing to any kids now. As a four-year-old sitting on an ugly little sofa with my Mum who I lived away from, though, the main character's story was all my own pain on-screen. We'd watch it and we'd have a little cry together – probably one of the only times we did cry together – and we'd feel the pain of loving each other so much and having to say goodbye. And oh man, when Dumbo's Mum cradles him through the bars of her jail and has to let him go, it's probably one of the saddest moments I can think of in cinema. Because it connected precisely with my experiences. Experiences that tiny me never really communicated externally but felt so vividly inside. That early loss of my Mum, viewed through the prism of a cartoon elephant, framed a lot of my feelings about loss through my life. Loss felt privately, painfully and in small moments nobody else got to touch.

Maybe it was the incomparable sadness of Disney, maybe it was me putting all my Mum sadness in the lockbox, but there came a point where I stopped wanting to look at things that connected me with those feelings, and if you're built like me, maybe you've felt this too. When you're engaged in a 24/7 struggle to keep the lid on your emotional Tupperware, the absolute last thing you want is to sit down and have it reflected back at you in your spare time. So I went into nature, and honestly, if you're struggling with a loss and want to find a place you can feel some things with freedom, I urge you to do the same. "I went into nature" sounds like I sold all my worldly goods and wandered into the woods in a loin cloth made of leaves, but I really just mean going outside. Taking train trips to wild places and brooding scenery that matches how you feel inside. There's something about standing at the top of a very big hill looking out at the sea when you're sad that just feels very, very right. It's the outdoors equivalent of Robyn's books of poetry – a place beaten by storms and weathered by weather, a vast and unending wilderness of complex things going on beneath the surface. It reminds us how small we are and how big the world is, and can separate us from general life enough to process some of what's going on. Maybe for you it'll be a calm meadow that helps you find peace in loss. Maybe dark mulchy woodland matches your temperament – they're all excellent. And for those of us who crave alone time to piece ourselves back together, nature's an incredible way of not only doing that, but of finding yourself outside of yourself as well. We introverts may not want to connect with people much through our losses, but we can still find ways to connect with the world.

Find your blanket

In amongst all the emotions and confusion and month-old sweatpants of loss, it can feel like you're supposed to be doing certain things, spending time in certain ways or reading certain books. And I'm here to tell you that you don't have to (except, errr, this one). Because I think there's a pressure to accept the help that lovely people want to give you, in whatever form it comes. To work your way through the meditation app, even though you hate it. To watch the really great documentary that helped your best friend, when all you want to do is stare at a wall. To go for a big walk because a book about loss told you to. But the truth is, it's about feeling your own way through it all, and letting people help you, yes, but not people-pleasing your way into letting them guide you down their own path. Sometimes it's OK to take the recommendation and not action it. So long as you can find your outlet or comfort blanket somewhere, you're doing OK. And it might take a while before you do. I'm still discovering things about my own reaction to loss, and that kind of fills me with wonder and hope that there are still better things to come. Your Wide World may not be made up of all-consuming representations of grief, but it might give you access to some of those difficult-to-reach emotions. The loss equivalent of teleportation. When you're so busy being anchored in the world that your reaction to loss escapes you, these things can help you get it back. They provide a little moment of solitude in which you can feel safe to be enveloped in grief for whatever you've lost. It's the power of taking time – even for a moment – to focus on a feeling, think it through, self-examine. Or if that seems like too much right now, to even just let yourself feel the feeling. Knowing I can do that now and not crumble into dust has been an unbelievably empowering part of my own journey through loss, another little brick in my own emotional house, and I hope a heckuvalot that it happens for you too.

This book is the little piece of culture that Robyn and I are putting back out into the world, and my hope is that it helps somebody like me, who made myself so invisible in my own loss, to feel connected to their emotional selves. Because it's real easy to distract and twiddle and lose sight of your needs, but when you get back to them, that's when the healing begins.

ACTION STATIONS

How can you connect with the world when you mainly want it to go away?

- Look around the house – is there anything that when you look at it just feels right? Go and spend some time looking at it and see where it takes you.

- Is there a song that reminds you of the thing or person you lost? If you can, pop that on, close your eyes and let whatever happens, happen.

- Type "landscapes" into Pinterest and see which ones feel most like your insides – you could even make a mental note to visit one of the places you've found when you have the energy.

ROBYN ON THE WIDE WORLD

From the extrovert who sees her loss everywhere

My Nan had Edith Piaf's "Non, je ne regrette rien" played at her funeral. My friend Shell will have Barbra Streisand and Donna Summer's "No More Tears (Enough is Enough)".[1] I will have Tim Curry belting out the *Rocky Horror* finale banger "I'm Going Home".[2] If you ask most people what song they want at their funeral, or their wedding, or as their theme tune, they'll know. Because it's my fervent view that art anchors our physical self in the world, gives us an iron-on identity and the tools to do some emotional excavation. I'd say art is the main thing that separates us from the rest of the species on the planet but there are the birds with the real jazzy nests and the fish who tart up their caves with endless shells and actually – all they're doing is spelling out their emotions too. Except their emotions are mainly "I'm feeling SEXY" or "STOP TRYING TO KILL ME". Which art sometimes addresses too. But very often it's LONELINESS. GRIEF. UNREQUITED LOVE.

"We tell ourselves stories in order to live." – Joan Didion

I've gone in on art straight off and really we need to backtrack and do some scene-setting. How you see your grief in the world is going to be linked to how you see yourself in the world, generally. Emma sees herself in a little cave, poking her head out from time to time, looking at it on Her Own Terms. She wants to figure it out solo, working from the raw

---

1 And a hologram of herself welcoming her guests with "Hello Darlings, I'm dead."

2 Now this is down on paper my family have absolutely no excuse to forget it. I also want "Baby, I'm Burning" by Dolly Parton as I'm wheeled into the crematorium oven.

materials all while hunkered down in a pastoral setting. I see the world like a *Where's Wally?* annual. But it's Where's Robyn? Colourful, dramatic, filled with people, me at the centre. That means I'm always on the hunt for whatever feeling I'm cultivating at that time. But, because I'm not terribly complex, I tend to eye up the most obvious representations. Sad tree = Robyn. Haunting song = Robyn. Depressing poetry = peak Robyn. And the thing that most irrefutably takes those feelings, reproduces them expertly on a canvas or page or large-scale robotic installation and holds it back up at us, is art. Art it is then. Though I'm also partial to standing on a windy shoreline looking exquisitely dramatic. But mainly, just art, 'cos you can't show off how good you are at standing on a windy shoreline looking exquisitely dramatic. Unless you photograph it. And then you're back at art again.

As you've probably gathered by now I am an extrovert. And a low-level narcissist. So seeing myself in things makes me think "Ahh OK, that's alright then. If [insert name of 75 per cent of poets and writers and painters and creators of most persuasions] created that masterpiece out of the jagged fragments of their broken heart then there must be a purpose to it. This crying woman before me was conjured up by a grief-stricken painter who felt a version of my pain AND was able to create a thing out of that that I am marvelling at hundreds of years later." It reframes loss as a perverse gift from the universe. A smashed pot you can make a breathtaking mosaic out of. Yes, you'd rather have the pot but unfortunately, all you've got is some glue and tracing paper to rectify this situation. I like to position my loss in the world in exactly that way, as part of an age-old tradition. Something natural and worthwhile. And then it isn't as hurty. Because to give things a purpose makes sense of them, even if it's a shitter, much sadder sense than – say – your brother being alive, your health being good, you still having the hope of reproducing or no one having run over your dog. Always better before but a slight improvement on crap if you repackage it. And you can repackage it in lots of ways re: the wider world.

Giving yourself an emotional enema

OK, that is a really gross and visceral way to introduce what I mean but it does sort of sum it up perfectly. When I was in the wars having first lost my Nan, it was hard to know when the emotions would pour out. In what order. And if I'd be in a safe place when they did. I felt absolutely and fully out of control. I put a lot of the highly damaging measures I've already mentioned in place to get a handle on it and they were not helpful at all. I implore you, don't try them. But what I did try and found really bloody effective was creating my own Dead Sad Disco. And it was AWESOME.

Club Cry-At-Your-Leisure is the same as any club really. There's also the Go Ballistic Ballroom for your angrier periods (plays metal) and The Overwhelmed-with-Euphoria Warehouse for moments you just want to revel in the good stuff. My list of comedy nightclub names is as endless as the kinds of emotion you might want to access but the crucial point is your name is on the list for Every. Single. One. When you step through the doors all bets are off. It's 2-4-1 Tuesday and the DJ is only taking your requests, baby. You can dance like billy-o, everything is heightened and no one is going to judge you for it the morning after. Mainly because Club Cry-At-Your-Leisure has a maximum capacity of one so the only person you get to judge is yourself. Now this all sounds a bit weird and psychedelic but you don't have to lock yourself in the bathroom and drop acid to do it. In fact, I'd actively discourage that. But what it basically is, is Viagra for the soul. For me that stimulant was a playlist of very, very depressing music. I'm talking Leonard Cohen, Willie Nelson, Eva Cassidy, Johnny Cash and, to my shame, U2. Appealing to my most base desires there but there was a time when I was locked in that bathroom with the shower on and Bono uttered the immortal lines:

> *We fight all the time*
> *You and I, that's alright*
> *We're the same soul*
> *I don't need, I don't need to hear you say*
> *That if we weren't so alike*
> *You'd like me a whole lot more*

All the muscles holding me upright suddenly relaxed and the heartbreak poured in. In that child-like crying that instantly flushes you out and leaves you feeling purged but also a bit desolate. Like after a big sick. The stuff that was making your stomach bubble is gone but now you just need to lie down for an afternoon. It provided the exact kind of schmaltzy Hallmark card basic-ness I needed back then. Just a "Look, that's you, that is" from Bono and my totally overworked brain could glance up from the emotional cryptic crossword it was failing to solve, sigh "Yep, so it is. Open floodgate number one, this is gonna get gushy", and for a little while I felt a bit less Absolutely Terrible. You can easily Blue Peter your own misery palace too, all you need is:

- Stuff that will make you cry
- A room with a lockable door
- Tissues[3]

It won't work for everyone. Emma wouldn't do it if you paid her. I see how it might feel forced and maybe inauthentic but if you're like me and your feelings are always bobbing just below the surface, desperate to get out and make a holy show of you, that kind of governance is glorious. The controlled explosion. Oh, that I was able to do all the time.

Whoever you are and whatever you're struggling with, it's worth a shot. The worst thing that's going to happen is your brain will be like, "Are you serious, you think I'm falling for that one?", you get a bit cross and resolve never to try it again. But maybe you'll find an outlet for the kaleidoscope of feelings trapped inside and that is something no one can argue against. Not even hands-off Hopkinson over there.

Hello, is it me you're looking for?

I could just finish this segment with "yes", but where would be the fun in that? I worry that this will seem super reductive but for a lot of people there is a glorious comfort in immersing yourself in art, whatever kind of loss you're experiencing. It's not a stretch to say that art has saved me. Or rather "the arts" saved me when I was going through a terrible loss. And that wasn't even the loss of Nan, it was the coincidental loss of my career. I was 24, I had worked in fashion since I had left uni, and I was managing and buying for a boutique in Nottingham. It was an extraordinary, once-in-a-lifetime opportunity that I didn't really realize was not in any way indicative of the actual fashion industry until I pulled the shutters closed one July

---

3   I am aware this also sounds like a goth masturbation manual.

That child-like crying that leaves you feeling purged but also a bit desolate

That child-like crying that leaves you feeling purged but also a bit desolate

That child-like crying that leaves you feeling purged but also a bit desolate

That child-like crying that leaves you feeling purged but also a bit desolate afternoon to go and watch my Nana die. I never returned to the life I had built in Nottingham or to that job because I moved into my grandad's remote farmhouse in rural Lancashire. I started all over again far too early and it quickly dawned on me I'd been working in some kind of Willy Wonka theatrical wonderland. My new position was the exact opposite of everything I'd experienced prior. Zero scope for creativity, processes coming out of your ears and no lovely relationship with the customers – just folding and spreadsheets and misery. I was so fucking sad because my career, and fashion in general, was and is my ultimate coat of armour. I'm really, really well-dressed in a look-at-me-I'm-confident-honestly, way. It was who I was and suddenly, I actually wasn't anymore and if I wasn't that then who was I except the amorphous blob that lay on the sofa crying about their bereavement?

Luckily, I was doing the Creative Writing MA (LJMU Class of 2011 – eh ohhhh) I keep mentioning, reading like mad and identifying so hard with otherness and loss that it felt like the only place I was understood. So I started to be like, "Maybe this is for me," because I like a quick win and it was a direct line to good-feeling city. I thought, "Maybe I can do this as a career." I saw an advertisement for ambassadors for a local literature organization and I convinced them to let me volunteer. And then I convinced them to actually hire me. And, as always happens to me, one of the directors, who is coincidentally one of the most inspirational women I know, also had that sweet I've-seen-some-shit sonar and heard my little mewls for help. And she gave me precisely the kind of support I needed at that time, which was being a total badass and pushing me *just* enough. That organization made me feel like I could use words to make a tangible difference to others and to myself and so I started to let go of my knotted little bundle of fashion sad and tug at the threads of my monster ball of bereavement angst. Doing something with art to benefit others while immersing myself in it fully made me feel part of a gang again. And I love me a gang. The Full Arts Immersion Recovery Method.

It made me read a tonne more than I was already reading. So, I got real familiar with some of the many, many books on loss. All the losses: death loss, career loss, health loss, identity loss, loss you've felt from birth 'cos you just don't connect with the wider world, loss of love, loss of battles... and continue ad infinitum. It made me see that loss is all around. To look at it like that is to feel like at least one other person gets you. You get to go up and examine something and suddenly up pops Club Cry-At-Your-Leisure, bad timing if you're in a gallery, great if you're in your reading nook. So if you want a fast-track to feelings of solidarity and sameness then go seek out some sad stuff, it'll paradoxically make you less sad. If you're like, "Whatever, this is tripe," I refer you to W. H. Auden's "Stop All the Clocks" in *Four Weddings*... As soon as John Hannah starts that poem, his love for Simon Callow becomes *our* love. *our* loss. We see *our* heartbreak. We recognize that futile desire for the world to just fucking acknowledge how everything is pointless and ruined now. The wish for it all to be shrouded in black. We are not alone. It's not high art or fantastically nuanced (the film, not the poem) but it illustrates my point exactly. So if that made you feel a bit better, you might want to try seeking out the kind of art that makes you feel seen.[4]

---

4 Sometimes it can be overkill though, like the time I took Emma to a spoken word play about dead cancer mums on the anniversary of her mum dying of cancer. Oh, how we cried. And made our fellow audience members, all five of them, jammed into a relatively small tent, feel really weird.

For me that has always been literature. Before I even got good and bereaved. I realize now that a large part of what drew me to study Classical Civilisation so vociferously and from, like, the tender age of 13, is that I felt at home with it. Because classical literature features a wildly disproportionate number of monstrous women and appalling mothers. Of people searching for something they know they'll never find or that would consume them if they did. I felt understood. Mourning for lost love was my old familiar because I'd been calling out for it since before I could remember. It was my first foray into art as therapy (though I didn't know it). It all spiralled out from there. Books that felt like Robyn were beloved. And helpful. And meted out to other friends in similar positions with limited success. Emma, for example, resisted my grief reading list for years but that's not her jam and I get that now. For her, it's like me holding up a photo of her mum on her deathbed and being like "LOOK AT IT." It's not good. But if it isn't highly triggering for you and you want to know what's on my loss reading list, here are some corkers:

- *The Year of Magical Thinking* by Joan Didion
- *Grief is the Thing with Feathers* by Max Porter
- *As I Lay Dying* by William Faulkner
- *H is for Hawk* by Helen Macdonald
- *The Father* by Sharon Olds
- *Time Lived, Without Its Flow* by Denise Riley
- *Norwegian Wood* by Haruki Murakami
- *Home Fire* by Kamila Shamsie
- And everything by ancient Greek playwright Euripides

All giving a spin on loss, in dramatically different ways. Be assured there's something for everyone out there, whatever your loss. The draw to put our experiences down on paper is pretty much universal so you're guaranteed to find something that speaks to you. Talking of the unrelenting urge to turn life into literature, I've segued myself perfectly into my next section...

Here I am!

I really enjoy that heading – that was the way I'd announce my entrance to any room in one of my old jobs. But my point here is that you can use art as therapy by shoving all the unfathomable stuff down on paper. For everyone on the planet or for the bottom of your desk drawer. Or make it into a pot. Or a painting. Or blow some glass into the shape of your grief (two halves of an anatomical heart, anyone?). When you're in a period of loss it can feel really bloody hard to muster up the energy to do pretty much anything, but putting yourself out into the world, and thinking about your new position there, it can be a godsend. To know that most great art found its genesis in something you have known so keenly, well that can be a very comforting notion. It's an elegy. A tribute to the magnitude of the thing you have lost and an acknowledgment of the comfortingly banal sameness of the human condition. You get to elevate your loss and also ground it in its inevitability. It is both extraordinary and very, very pedestrian.

I did this by attending my writing course and haranguing my poor, mainly very patient classmates with sad chapters about a motherless boy. To illustrate my point, here is how my novel opened:

I think the most important thing that anyone needs to know about me is that I have no mother. That and I'm in love with my best friend. Sometimes I think that's because I don't have a mother.

I was thirteen when she went. We lost her in the summer. I still remember the rattle of her chest and the burn for it all to end. Rise... fall... rise... fall... pause. Everyone held their breath... rise. She asked my father for help so many times, never once said a word to me, just squeezed my hand when I said bad things, angry at the mob round the fucking bed, engulfing her, all about themselves. I was so small it was hard to slot in.

And any member of my family will know this scene intimately because it is the last few hours of my Nan's life. I wasn't 13 but I felt too small to squeeze in. She didn't say a word to me, but she'd already said a goodbye I now have tattooed on my heart.[5] If I let myself hear her cry out for help my throat physically closes up. It was undoubtedly too close to be good writing at the time. But my god did it help. To remould it into something I could catch a hold of was incredible. By putting it at arm's length I could look at it, make sense of it, render it less dangerous. So thank you for the two years' worth of free therapy, my fellow students, and one lovely teacher who, you guessed it, sonar-ed the shit out of me. I call her Mummy Bear and I won't be made to feel strange about that.

My point is: if you are so inclined then use your loss. Put it out into the world like you're able to paint your own

---

5 Metaphorically and physically. One of the last things she said to me is tattooed on my ribcage, next to my heart. You can become the art.

Ophelia with it. Rage up a *Guernica* or "Do Not Go Gentle into That Good Night" or break hearts by drafting *Stones in His Pockets* or *Up*[6] or whatever makes it feel useful and malleable and manageable. Turn it all outwards and let it shine into the world and just like that, you're safe. The Medusa's head of misery can no longer turn you to stone and, Brucey Bonus, it even provides you with a little emotional weaponry. Something good can be hewn out of the very worst of situations, like carving something out of a magnificent tree knocked down in a blasted bloody storm. IF you're that way inclined, that is.

---

6 Please no one write another *Up*, I genuinely couldn't take it. I'd sick up my heart.

ACTION STATIONS
Creating the festival of you.

- Get Googling. For books on loss. Or exhibitions. Or films. There's so much stuff out there so start having a look. You may like it, you may hate it, but you don't know until you try.

- Make a playlist or equivalent collection of things that provide you with an emotional release. It's good to have a go-to place where you know you can connect with the bottled-up emotions.

- Try writing, creatively. Fictionalize things. Sometimes it's a way of tricking your mind into divulging the stuff it doesn't want to offer straight up. Or it gives you a break from real life. It might be rubbish but that doesn't matter.

Dr Sheetal Says...

Some people grieve privately and want it to be theirs only whilst some need everyone to know, so that they can share it and seek reassurance. Using your loss to create something meaningful or taking it out and examining it away from the goggles of grief turns it into some sort of semi-fiction that doesn't feel too intrusive.

The point is that you are bringing it out of you and into the world and trying to experience it in a less threatening way. If it feels too hard, try again when you're feeling less vulnerable. Perhaps then you may start to realize a path to processing your loss. But take your time, there's no rush if it doesn't feel right yet. The important thing is that you are giving it some time to percolate into the unknown and begin to experiment with managing any difficult feelings that arise.

Another important thing is that you don't stay alone in this loss, whether you choose to share this with people or yourself. Don't block the emotions; they need to be processed and attended to – this might sound daunting and it might take a while to unravel what the loss means to you, others and the world.

Sharing with others in art can feel like you're bonding with a community who understands, but not purely based on the loss you share, and so this doesn't define you. Sometimes we need that. Knowing other people have found their way through stuff too can be very powerful. For those who are less socially inclined and would rather connect with the world than others, the natural art of the outdoors has been shown to be wonderfully therapeutic. Sometimes we can lose sight of this as we deal with the world and all its practicalities (sorting a will, applying for new jobs, looking after a newborn). Self-reflection can come in solitude or with others and they both give value.

FORGIVE

Green-eyed boy,
I write this from where you left off   *the land of the living*   so called.

And how do you like your digs are you somewhere now bumping dark riddims
cut with a thread of light?

What a time to be alive *everyone's going on spare not just my life going on pear*
have I told you about this recurring nightmare:

a hammer   coming down   on a tree stump my hand   waiting on the stump for the blow?

I learned of your passing as I dressed for a wedding
shifting the knot of my tie I said *ok* – marvelling

at the way a stock phrase insinuates itself the way certain man spread
to fill a space –

we hadn't spoken in months   had I known the words *bruv, what is good*
would be the last words

of our correspondence I would have told you how the table and chairs in your
mother's kitchen rebuilt me.

I would have asked if you remembered the day we heard krytstal klear on rinse and
glimpsed joy long enough to dance.

"Because bereavement has been a fact of my life from a relatively early age I have always been fascinated by death, mourning, and grief as a subject for writing and for art generally. For me writing begins as a preoccupation with a particular idea, phrase, or image. Once they move me, I find it hard to let certain stimuli go. The deaths of those I love are particularly resonant, then, because writing through that grief is a way of extending kinship across the existential chasm between living and death."

Poet Kayo Chingonyi on the power of creativity through loss, in response to his poem *Forgive*

TREAT YO'SELF

When you're going through a loss, looking after yourself can feel like studying rocket science, on a unicycle, while you're on fire. Here's how to take care of the big and little things to keep yourself functioning.

Emma: Self-care is hard at the best of times, so when you're going through a loss it's probably at the end of a very long emotional list. We were both very much not treating ourselves through our big losses.

Robyn: I mean, I barely put pants on.

Emma: I put all my pants on, plus lipstick, earrings and heels, to show I was OK. Do you think it's because we just didn't know any better?

Robyn: Yeah, for sure. And, for me, it just felt like such a lot of effort. I lay down. You really ploughed on with life – that's why I thought you were OK. Or had gone mad.

Emma: The second one is probably right.

ROBYN ON TREATING YO'SELF
Notes on self-care from the queen of self-indulgence

Thinking of things that make the unbearable nature of loss a bit more bearable can be really bloody hard, wherever you sit on the introvert/extrovert scale. There are things that feel too insubstantial, like a spa day. There are things that feel too massive to even consider, like a pilgrimage along the road to Santiago. There's advice that is really accurate but just sounds dumb: eat some food, dude, it'll power you up like Super Mario after a mushroom.[1] When putting underwear on is literally the pinnacle of your daily achievements, treating yourself can feel so wildly out of reach that it's laughable.

If I've lost something, the first thing I do is get massively overwhelmed, have a full-body freak out, lie down and become unable to do anything. It's like I short circuit. Ask Jamie. I just cannot deal. It's one of my worst qualities. I dwell on that thing in an all-encompassing way. It's a real treat for everyone around me. I'm either incommunicado or totally overcommunicado in that I cannot shut up about the thing I lost, how I lost it, how it felt to lose it, how I could hypothetically replace it, etc. There's a mania to it and it detaches me from the real world and I just pop inside myself and implode.

I've done it with loss of places, people, friendships. Man, oh man. FRIENDSHIPS. I have mourned the loss of friendships harder than I've mourned the end of romantic relationships. Someone needs to be talking more about how life-changing closing a door on a friendship is because that

---

1 Don't just eat mushrooms.

shit is tough. I've grieved for the end of love affairs, my sense of self, my sense of security, the lot. I'm actually doing it as I write. I've experienced loss of freedom, as have we all now with various national lockdowns, and it sent me completely into freefall. The loss of community and scope for joy was unbearable. I started this wave of confinement full of woe, unable to do anything meaningful. Sitting down watching TV for between four and fourteen hours straight because that's all my brain could face. Mushy nothing. Spoon feed me societal gruel. I wanted the world to be manageably grey, thank you very much. HD will send me under.

All these losses are responded to on the Robyn sliding-scale of hysteria. And can I just clarify right here, that this shit is hereditary. My Nanny Al,[2] who was a squishy marshmallow of a woman with nerves strung tighter than a violin bow, passed on her Olympian levels of anxiety to me. When my grandad went to fight in World War II, my Nanny Al "lost her legs", which is not to say she lost her actual walkers, but she was so completely overwhelmed with the pre-emptive sense of loss that she just... lost the use of her legs. She was hospitalized for it. It was a Very Bad Time. I have the same habit of fast-forwarding to Doomsville, though less intense. So, when the actual worst happens, initially, I am actually fucked. I completely lose my head. Though not, up to now, my legs.

The first few days after Nan died I thought, nightly "If I could just die in my sleep, that would be super." I told my job I wasn't going back because my grandad handily gave me an out by asking me not to leave him when we walked out of that hospice. I was like "Bingo – I'm taking him at

---

2 The same great grandmother that willed herself to fade away after her husband died.

his literal word." I rang my lovely boss and explained, Jamie packed up our stuff and we moved home. I didn't have to do a thing. So I didn't. I lay flat. I entertained a lot of very wonderful friends who came to check I was OK. And resolved to shun anyone who didn't. I ate too little. I fell asleep all the time because what else is there to do? In that way, maybe I did self-care myself because I got to do all the things that made me feel OK. Unfortunately, the things that made me feel OK were being slightly anorexic and a bit depressed, and I had the luxury of doing them loads. I let all the things I loved to do, and that made me feel like me, slip away because #effort. I wore no make-up and didn't enjoy dressing up or being a pantomime dame, which is pretty much my main schtick. Imagine a bare-faced Dame Edna but not the jolly Barry Humphries version. Or Ru Paul but not Ru Paul in a Klein, Epstein & Parker suit. Ru Paul in that surgical face stocking he wore in the lockdown finale. Sad, resigned and a bit ridiculous. Imagine that thoroughly depleted version of them, wearing their dead relative's jumper for the fourth day on the trot. Intensely fragrant but lacking in everything else.

In losing my sense of identity and becoming Grief Girl, I lost any feelings of responsibility to look after myself because *I wasn't myself.* I couldn't even begin to fathom how to get back to that woman because I could barely work out how to put my knickers on the right way round. But, with the remarkable gift of hindsight, I can see ways in which I could have been a little kinder, found things to do that seemed manageable and strategies I could have gently introduced.

I could barely work out how to put my knickers on the right way round.

Vegetate to accumulate

OK this sounds counterintuitive BUT self-care can be about sitting still for a second, assessing what you're doing, its impact on you, and getting comfortable with your current limitations. It's about cutting yourself some slack and saying "It's OK that I can't be a superhero today." I realized the amazing potential of doing something so-familiar-it's-basically-second-nature pretty young. There is an unparalleled comfort in knowing exactly what the next line is. Left to its own devices, your bastard mind can easily go into freefall so I found it really useful to give mine incredibly simple tasks and little distractions. Here's an example. When I was nine my mum left. But, in an avant garde twist, she kicked me, my dad and my seven-year-old brother out of the family home. So far, so traumatic.

Because, as you've probably gathered, my Nan was a big, bacon-sandwich-wielding, just-enough-love-giving port in a storm, she took in her son-in-law and her shell-shocked grandchildren. We all lived smooshed together, pretending not to fall apart. When you're nine, you don't know you're falling apart but I can now see that the frequent crying until I hyperventilated was actually panic attacks, and the years of pretty terrible insomnia weren't entirely normal. When I woke up, nightly, at about 1am, I would occupy myself by catastrophizing everything, imagining ghosts and monsters and unknowable foes, so lay pranging out until it became light. It was sub-optimal. BUT two things would soothe my racing brain. One was waking up someone in the house so the monsters wouldn't get me and the other was Roald Dahl audiobooks – my first foray into self-care, though I didn't know it at the time. Because I was nine. I listened to *The BFG*, *Matilda* and *Fantastic Mr Fox* over and over and over. Just having words in the background to not really focus on was a lullaby. I was distracted *just enough* to nod off. My mind had a task and by Jove, it was going to sleep on the job. The repetitive nature of things and the easy familiarity can be just the tonic. I've spoken to other friends who've lost something and they've said something similar. That they're only able to do things that take the minimal of effort and that is OK. There are times to challenge yourself and there are times to not. Trust you know yourself enough to see when to deploy either. When Nan went, I basically only watched very old sitcoms that I knew all the words to. And, weirdly, as my uncle had lent me his portable DVD player, the Katherine Heigl not-masterpiece, *27 Dresses*. I, to this day, do not know the plot to that film. I suspect there isn't one. So, pick up a book that doesn't challenge you, switch to a box set that doesn't ask you to concentrate, pop on an app specially designed to destress, like Calm or Headspace, and give your tired old brain a rest – it's earned it.

Let's go outside (sing it, damn you)

I stagnated a lot. A lot, a lot. But being outside was really helpful for me. Luckily, I was living on a farm that is almost a mile away from either neighbour and so was able to do it whenever I fancied. But I didn't at first, because I was busy just doing the basics in order not to waste away to nothing. If you're an extrovert, any activity that doesn't involve an audience or an outcome can feel kind of pointless, so being outdoorsy might not feel like your natural habitat. But that's why you have to do it in a way that suits you, which is likely not to be a freeform solo amble. For me I like to engage with the outdoors in three ways:

1. A long, long blustery beach walk with a friend where we do some SOUL SEARCHING.
2. Running.
3. Fishing. Yeah, fishing. Didn't expect that one, right?

So, if you're in a muddle and heading out seems totally pointless, give it a point, it can be helpful. The first approach is self-explanatory. The second is absolute gold as it cheats your brain into feeling better. It's the lazy man's route to a little moment of euphoria. Even if you're sad, your body tricks you into not moping through a big run, or any form of exercise. You might do a big cry but you'll be doing it at speed and it will probably feel amazing to get it out. So if you can offer yourself that remedy then do. Exercise also gives you time to distract yourself and a place to go where other people aren't. Podcasts on a run/walk/trampolining/ yoga session gives your mind something to focus on and you can pitch it at whichever tempo you need. Ambient noise or enthralling thriller, the choice is yours.

And now we come to fishing. I love fishing. The fishing I do rarely involves catching anything, as when I do I am guaranteed to freak out, make someone else deal with it, throw it back and shudder for the next half an hour about the terrible thing that just happened. Because, actually, converse to everything I said before, fishing for me was a way to be in nature and not have an action. I mean I did, I was fishing. But it's more akin to meditation. You sit very still and concentrate on nothing but the movement of water. Time is irrelevant. You are just *being*. The problem is I can't just *be* without *doing* but that's completely counterintuitive, so I tricked myself by having the absolute minimum of doings to do. I was quiet and focused – a state

I've rarely experienced except, weirdly, at the aquarium. I absolutely loved it. I'm sure there are other outdoor activities that would provide the same absorbing tranquillity. Twitching maybe? Cloud watching? The point is, give a meditative pursuit a bash. Find some reason to be peacefully immobile. Give yourself a whisper of something to hook in on so your mind doesn't take the chance to race. I never thought I'd say it but it can be incredibly helpful to just be… static.

Go on tour

Back to the old proactive, jump-on-the-horse-and-ride-it-fast-to-OK-town method. When you are in a period of loss, everything around you can remind you that life is a bit terrible. Your stupid kitchen is the same stupid kitchen. The walk to the shop is woefully predictable. WHERE IS THE WONDER IN THE WORLD? Well, I can tell you where it isn't – in your house, probably. Sometimes it's OK to say "I'm booking my tired body and my even tireder mind a trip." I'm talking about an actual physical excursion. Could be a weekend in a tent in Llandudno, could be a month in Mexico, could be a year travelling the globe. Sometimes you need a change of scenery so marked that not even your blasted subconscious can pipe up and say "That mountain looks a bit like my ex-boyfriend." It doesn't Kaasni, unless, *maybe* you're looking at Mount Rushmore and your ex was heavily into historical re-enactments. Sometimes it's good to remind yourself that while the world can be an awfully cruel place, it's also incredible. That there are still many, many things to marvel at. That the sun on your face can warm your heart for a minute. That you can just bathe in otherness for a bit.

A few years ago, I left a job that involved working for a chaotic tyrant who gaslighted the buggery out of any of her staff that didn't want to be her a. closest ally or b. substitute child. I massively spun out. I was anxious to the point of thinking I might have to be hospitalized. I had become comfortable in that toxic environment and to leave felt absolutely terrifying as I'd just bought a flat and in it found a little normality after five straight years of living with a parent or in-law. And I was about to risk all that to move to another role that maybe wouldn't work out. It all seemed absolutely the highest stakes and I was convinced I'd ruin everything. Unfortunately, the next job was even worse but that is not the point. The point is, I had a holiday booked that my lovely pals had got me for my thirtieth birthday. As much as I thought I might go catatonic in Sardinia and have to be ferried around in a sedan chair, that break from London was transformative. Yes, I was still having all-consuming black thoughts, crying for no reason twice a day, doing a lot of mindfulness and lying down 'cos I was overwhelmed pretty much all the time. But I also had moments of wonder and escapism and mental rest that I wouldn't have got in my usual surroundings. In a very basic sense, absolutely everything was different and sometimes that is glorious. For the world around you to feel loud and bombastic and like it doesn't give a shit about your pain, but in a way that won't make you furious. You can't be furious at arancini.[3] You can take this at a micro level and go to an exhibition, a theme park, to see an action film or visit some botanical gardens. But I do think there's something about getting in the car/train/bus/plane and knowing you won't be home for a little bit that's really excellent for the soul.

---

3 Unless you're lactose intolerant.

Let them eat cake

I know I give it loads about not pushing yourself and going at your own pace and using your intuition and things but also, there are ways to push yourself. Push yourself to do something that you know has brought you joy in the past. It can be as simple as eating a really shiny item of patisserie, or watching the snooker, or putting on some lipstick, or getting a haircut, or going to a spa (yes, I know I said that was stupid but it might not be stupid at some point in the journey), or go for dinner or anything. Try nourishing yourself. It might sound mad but maybe diarize an alert for, say once a fortnight, to try a thing you loved again. Start small, you don't need to career straight back into base-jumping, but test yourself. If it feels too much, you could task a friend or relative with coming up with a cheery challenge once a month.

This is very much another tried-and-tested thing for me. When we moved into the farm dad was basically smashed to smithereens[4], my Nan and her sister, my Auntie Sue, and sometimes their mum, my Nanny Al, would host The Friday Night Club. Real club, real name, real awesome.[5] They had correctly assumed that the environment we were living in, the chaos and the mania and the fights and the crying, was all completely intolerable for young children. So once a week they would take us out and do something totally escapist with us. Bowling or crazy golf or an unforgettable night of making peg dolls at Nanny Al's bungalow that feels like a scene from a film, I remember it so clearly. I am so

---

4 Physically and emotionally, he shattered his pelvis, SHATTERED IT. You can feel that in your (pelvis) bones, right?
5 As I read that back and let the fact my family came up with a happiness club with high-octane excursions sink in, all I can say is: breeding tells.

grateful that they cared enough to know we were hurting and that they decided to do something about it, that it makes me weep to this day. We were very lucky to have such amazing women around us. That their emotional intuition was so in-tune. They saved us. And, the point I'm getting at, is they took the reins and let us have a little go at things we usually liked once a week. Didn't matter if we hated it. No pressure. Just someone flashing some things you liked under your nose and seeing what you make of it. You'll be surprised what connects. So be active in re-familiarizing yourself with joy. See if you can let it in again. No pressure if you can't, it will show its face one day.

Get a dog

As it sounds.

So there you have my self-care chapter. It's not exhaustive, it's scant in clearly actionable suggestions. It's an extrovert's nightmare. But I think what it's trying to say is – do a little of what makes you happy, whether you want to or not. You deserve moments of rest and comfort, so seek them out wherever you can.

ACTION STATIONS
Little things that make a big difference.

- Order yourself something – a candle, a crossword book, a hair mask, an airfix model – off the internet. No need to even leave the house. Try to use that thing to relax yourself. Limit the spend to a small amount so you aren't stressed if it goes in the bin.

- Ask a friend to arrange a day of fun. Or an afternoon. Or an hour. Sometimes not having to think and to be obliged to enjoy something is actually really excellent.

- Make/buy/order in and eat one thing you loved a week and see if it still brings you joy. The process will give you a rest from relentless thinking and cake tends to remain delicious, even if you are absolutely bereft.

EMMA ON TREATING YO'SELF

Notes on self-care from the one who thought she didn't deserve it

If you're an introvert like me, your instinct through loss will probably be to hibernate away from people and recharge. And if the thought of asking a friend to organize a day of fun for you makes you want to set fire to everything, I'm here to give you some alternatives that you can do *all by yourself* – the sweetest three words that ever there were.

How well-equipped you are to look after yourself will have a lot to do with your state of mind. When my Mum died, self-care wasn't at the top of my CV. I was 26 and didn't like myself very much. At the beginning of a career I never thought I'd get to have, I was fake-it-till-you-make-it-ing, dealing with imposter syndrome, trying to adult correctly and surviving largely on apples and strong black coffee. In those times where you're forging ahead into territories unknown, having anchor points you can refer back to and remember who you are can feel like a little life raft. So, before she popped off, I would call my Mum on my lunch breaks and we would laugh and joke and connect in a way I didn't feel I could with other people. That was always the way for us - we were peas in a strangely-shaped pod full of warmth and laughter and ease. So losing her meant I also lost those little moments of grounding and reconnection. And if you're going through the loss of a relationship, an estrangement or saying goodbye to a much-loved career, you might feel that too – sometimes the very thing you've lost is the thing that used to nourish you, so you're having to not only navigate it no longer being there, but also work out how to fill in the gaps it used to fill, as well. It's the old adage about breakups, that the one person you'd usually turn to for support isn't there anymore. And it is absolute balls.

My lasting wish for you, as you're reading this, is that you find ways to navigate your own loss that don't leave you a shell of a person. Post-loss was not a good time in Emma Land, and I'm still undoing the knots I got myself into, many years later. So grab your shopping trolley and let's browse the aisles of the Self-Care Supermarket to find ways to avoid being a sad jelly with a hard outer shell, and do some good stuff for yourself. Some of the good stuff here might feel the same as what you saw in Robyn's bit – find time for yourself, go outside – but the purpose and reason behind them, how you feel while you're doing them, and how they help you to process will be something quite different. This is the Introvert's Self-Care Citymapper – it should get you to the same places, but using a slightly different route. A route with fewer people on it.

Be your own safe space

First things first: please know that you don't need to be OK. If the swinging log of loss has knocked you off your perch, let yourself sit on the floor for a bit while the little cartoon birds fly around your head. Healing takes time, and you can't fast-forward time. So take days off work, turn off notifications on your phone, let friends know you're out of action for a while – you don't even have to tell them why if you don't want to. But the first part of *The People-Pleasing Introvert's Complete Guide to Self-Care Through Loss* (niche) is to make time for yourself. Yes, life is busy, yes, there are things you feel you *should* be doing, but taking a little time to focus on you is going to make getting back to that life a whole lot easier. And cry. If you feel the tears coming, cry. Wherever you are.

it will take time to heal from a loss
it will take time to heal from a loss
it will take time to heal from a loss
it will take time to heal from a loss
it will take time to heal from a loss
it will take time to heal from a loss
it will take time to heal from a loss
it will take time to heal from a loss
it will take time to heal from a loss
it will take time to heal from a loss
it will take time to heal from a loss
it will take time to heal from a loss
it will take time to heal from a loss
it will take time to heal from a loss
it will take time to heal from a loss
it will take time to heal from a loss
it will take time to heal from a loss
it will take time to heal from a loss
it will take time to heal from a loss
it will take time to heal from a loss
it will take time to heal from a loss
it will take time to heal from a loss

and you are worthy of that time

Nobody will think badly of you for it – when was the last time you saw somebody crying and thought, "What an idiot"? I spent so long burying my emotions that sometimes even to this day I struggle to get to them and let them out. But I know now that if I don't, I'm right back in Anxiety Town, where the cocktails are adrenaline and the only music is sudden loud noises and bagpipes.

You might be one step ahead of where I was through my Big Loss and have an actual self-care routine you rely on, and if you do, that's great – sticking to familiar things can be a really good way to ground yourself. If you're finding it difficult to do the things you'd usually do to make yourself feel better, though, it can make you feel even more out of sorts. If that happens, it's totally fine – notice it, maybe grab a pencil and write it down. In fact, writing stuff down is one of my all-time favourite ways to practise self-care. Introverts tend to live a rich internal life, which makes us wonderfully insightful in good times, but in tough times can leave us with a swirling mess of emotions in our heads that are difficult to pin down. And our brains throw up little nuggets at the weirdest moments – I can't tell you how many times I've found myself on a busy street when something pops into my head I don't quite have the brain power to deal with. An extrovert might simply mention it to the person they are with, but an introvert will likely want to mull it over for a bit before they get it out for public consumption. So, if getting your emotional crown jewels out in public makes you want to hide in a cupboard, try writing. Or something next to writing, like drawing or music or sticking beads onto card. It might seem strange to an introvert at first, but it can help to get everything out of your head into semi-cohesive thoughts. It means you have to sift through them properly to find the right words/brushstroke/chords/bead adhesive. It can help to bring focus to yourself and your state of mind, and feel completely cathartic. But if you hate writing and crafts, try another thing. Whatever helps you work through the feelings to stop them swirling around your head, do that. You could write about a moment you felt something and what you were doing in it. You could write three words about how you're feeling today. Or you could even try a little journaling. Taking a moment each day to jot down thoughts, check in with yourself and see how you're doing can be just the thing you need to help make sense of the world. How and when you do your journaling will be unique to you. I favour first thing in the morning, from bed, before my brain is working properly and usually before I've spoken to anybody else. I find that if I wait too long, I'm distracted by other things and struggle to focus. Try writing down how you're feeling, or, if you're not sure how you're feeling, write whatever comes into your head, following that along until you finally get somewhere. It could be, "I really don't want to do this today" or, "All I can think about is waffles" but if it's honest and true it'll usually lead to the thing your brain's stuck on. You can buy whizzy journals with different sections and moods to fill out and productivity tips and colour coding and if that's your bag, great – find the thing that works for you.

Another mega-helpful way of writing is letters. Not like pen pals – though do that if you like – but more like writing to the person or thing you lost. Sometimes my therapist will try to get me to role play talking to somebody who isn't in the room. "What would you like to say to them?" she'll ask. And I'll sit there mute and embarrassed, because it's just not my bag, but give me a piece of paper and I'm away. They're not letters you ever send – they're one-sided conversations that help to get you thinking about how you really feel. It could be an apology for stealing your ex-friend's shoes, it could be a love letter to a lost partner or an angry tirade to the parent who walked out on you, but there's something about that feeling of indirect contact that really frees up the mind and helps you access your honest thoughts and feelings about a thing. So don't hold back. Get it all out. Then you can choose whether to keep it or burn it.[6] Or do what I did and drunkenly hand it to a friend on a night out after your therapy session. Like we keep saying, loss is complicated.

The quiet life

If you're already feeling overwhelmed by the world, self-care can just feel like another thing on the to-do list and make you want to hire a personal assistant you can outsource it all to. So I'm going to come out in praise of sitting still. In the bath, outside on a bench, sprawled on the local park. Because when you sit still your mind can catch up with itself. No phone, no TV screen, just you and your brain. Nobody ever had an emotional revelation watching *Die Hard* (probably). And, like Robyn, I've discovered the powers of a mild distraction to help you do it. It becomes almost a meditation. If you struggle to sit still, try lying down somewhere quiet, put headphones on playing music you like and hold something to fiddle with in your hands. Let your mind wander. Relax your jaw. Take it slow – if you can do a minute of that in the beginning, that's good going. Write down anything that popped into your head afterwards and then do something lovely for yourself as a reward. Because

---

6 If you set fire to anything, please do it really, really carefully and away from anything else flammable, like gasoline or that shell suit you've been hanging onto just in case.

the truth is, if you're finding self-care difficult, it feels like work. And, like most work, you're more likely to do it if there's something nice at the end of it, whether that's a fat paycheck or a giant cookie.

One of my therapist's favourite things to ask is: what would feel like relief? If you're feeling overwhelmed, or can't work out how you feel, the chances are you're all knotted up and tense. So take a moment and focus on what relief would feel like. Take a breath. Let your neck relax, let your shoulders drop, and try to relax your belly and chest. Then think about what would feel good that day. Maybe a whole day of sitting in front of the telly with your phone off. Maybe a misty walk. Maybe reading, baking – whatever gives you that relaxed feeling in your chest – carve out some time in your week to do that. Learning what relief feels like can really help you navigate your feelings of loss.

Probably the easiest-access thing to do is to go for some outside time by yourself. Where you live will have some bearing on how easy this is, but, for my introvert crew, my recommendation is to go to the quietest, most brooding spot you can find and amble around in it. If off-road walking is open to you, go feel the grass underfoot; if you need to stay path-bound, go find the spot with the most open view and spend some time there. Look around you, breathe fresh air, smell the smells, look at big scenery, breathe it in. To me, there's nothing so nourishing as being in nature when you're hurty inside, but wherever you are, taking time to just mosey and think can be a tonic. No music, no podcasts, no social media, just you, doing something great for yourself. The movement helps to burn off anxiety's adrenaline, the headspace helps you sift through some feelings, the scenery is a change from the cushion you've had your face buried in for the past week – it really is a win-win. If for whatever reason going for alone time outdoors isn't an option, it's fine to ask for some alone time when you get there. It's always fine to ask for alone time. I need to get that on a T-shirt.

After all that outdoor time, you might want a little sleep. Or a big sleep that lasts a million years and which you'll wake up from in perfect mental health. Wouldn't that be wonderful? But, frequently, for the anxious-minded, when you need it most, sleep can be elusive. And when you're in the cycle of poor sleep, even knowing it's close to bedtime can get the old anxiety ramping up. My brain likes to take me off to bed, lie me down and then cycle through all the things I've ever regretted doing in life. The stupid thing I said at a party, the time I let a friend down, the conversation I had that day that I could've handled better. Thanks, brain. And then I'll get down to worrying about sleep itself, before finally getting angry with myself for not sleeping and eventually falling into some kind of fitful slumber at an unearthly hour in the morning. Sound familiar? Think we've all been there at some point. So I say sleep, if you can. But don't pressure yourself. Grab yourself some sleepy tea, book an evening massage, do some breathwork – it's about creating a relaxing environment your brain can unwind in. And if right now that's a struggle, try not to give yourself a hard time. Once you deal with the emotional bits that are keeping you awake, great sleep will be yours. Oh yes, it will be yours.

The same thing goes for food – if you're like I was and are struggling to make room for actual, edible nourishment in your day, try creating an environment where you're set up for success. Because nothing is guaranteed to befuddle clear thinking quite like not eating. So, plan your meals, make sure you have food at home that you feel able to prepare. It doesn't need to be cordon bleu – it might just be something you can bung in the oven each night, but having it to hand means you're far more likely to actually put food in your mouth. And if you hate cooking with a fiery passion, you could try asking a friend to help, or even try having meal boxes delivered. So long as there's food and you're eating it regularly, you're doing pretty well. It's about energy, yes, but it's also about taking time to give yourself nourishment – that symbolic moment of feeding yourself reminds you that you're showing up for yourself, prepared to spend time making sure you get through this.

Spreadsheets and self-care

Your levels of self-care and what you actually need through loss will be totally unique to you and your situation. Looking back on my own Big Loss, I know that having systems in place to look after myself would've helped me stay on track and stopped me spiralling quite so out of control. But only you know what you need – it's about taking a serious look at that and choosing to do something nice for yourself, whether that's base-level survival or a spot of indulgence. Nobody's saying you need to be leaving the funeral early to go and do a face mask, but it's important to understand how you're working and what messages you're sending your brain about how important you are in it all. And I'm here to tell you that you *are* important. That you deserve kindness from yourself. That it will take time to heal from a loss and you are worthy of that time.

Whether you're one day or ten years into your loss, this, right now, is your opportunity to do one right thing for yourself. Even if you have never put yourself first before. Even if you feel your struggle is an overreaction. Even if you're the last person you think deserves that effort — this is your time to stop, take stock and work through some of what's there. Because if you don't, nothing is going to change. Loss — any loss — is an upheaval, and if you try to just continue on with business as usual, you're going to burn out. Nobody is a machine, and we all have times we need a bit more love from ourselves than usual. You gotta cut yourself some slack and give the hurting part of you a bit of air time; a chance to be heard, and a chance to be loved by you.

ACTION STATIONS

When life feels too busy for self-care, how can you make yourself a priority?

- Schedule your me-time. Just like you put your appointments and meetings in your diary, plan in designated times for you to focus on yourself, cook dinners, journal. If it's built into your day, you're more likely to do it.

- Scatter little sensory touch points through your day as a reminder that you're taking care of yourself. Light a favourite candle while you work, wear your most huggable jumper, spritz your most comforting scent.

- Any time you catch yourself giving sad-you a hard time, pause, take a breath and then say, "I matter, I'm worth caring for." Even if you don't believe it at first, even hearing those words said about yourself can have a profound effect.

Dr Sheetal Says...

When life has knocked you for six – for reasons of loss or otherwise – and when you don't even see the point of getting out of bed in the morning, it can feel counterintuitive to get out and do things.

Start small and manageable, otherwise you put yourself at risk of overwhelming yourself into thinking you can't handle it. Routine helps, or mapping out your week so you can see things clearly and have things to look forward to. In your routine, add a) something you enjoy, even if it is just a warm bubble bath or eating your favourite snack; b) something where you might learn, like an instrument or a new language; and then c) work, do something like sorting your flat or going to work, or write a book! Make some time for the activity and say it out loud, write it down, put a reminder in your phone so that you are forced to think about doing it and don't get lost into a vacuum of watching trash TV all day. But if you do, it's OK. Try again tomorrow, or the day after.

If you can, exercise can be a great way to raise endorphins – running is my own personal way to destress. These activities can be a form of mindfulness and meditation where we focus on the task at hand.

Take time to think about your values, what matters to you, and how you make more space for those things in your life. And finally, be kind to yourself. Eat, sleep and show yourself your worth, in the same way you might have done before the loss. As blunt as it may sound, nothing will truly change if nothing is done, and a little effort is required even if all you want to do is hide away. Once you have made that effort, reward yourself, because no matter how small the action was, I am sure it was bloody difficult. Read yourself mantras like, "I am worth it" whilst smiling at yourself in the mirror, until you finally believe it.

At first I struggled with getting older. It felt strange after a lifetime of it that people weren't gawking, beeping their horns, or whistling for me to come over.

I didn't realize how much my self-esteem was dependent on the aggressive adoration of others.

Now I recognize it. Now I know what bullshit that was. Now I know I don't need that anymore. Now I'm free.

I know now that we don't become obsolete if no one is looking. We don't disappear if others don't find us attractive. Now we know we don't need validation or approval from others. Now we are free.

Blogger Natalie Lee of *Style Me Sunday* on the peculiar freedoms of losing youth

MISTY WATERCOLOUR MEMORIES

Nothing is ever truly lost, because it lives on through us. And how you keep it going will be totally unique to you, whether you talk about it all the time, or remember it in private moments.

Robyn: I think the thing I have that reminds me most of my Nan is this ring she used to wear. It's like a little diamond ring and whenever we were out I'd be like, "Go on, let me wear the diamonds, Nan." And she would. So now I wear it and it's like she's there every day.

Emma: That is bloody wonderful. When my Mum died I think I put all her stuff in a literal box.

Robyn: You did! I wore my Nan's shoes compulsively until they fell apart.

Emma: And then you sort of do a mini-mourn for the thing that fell apart and the memories and the person attached to the thing all over again.

Robyn: But if it's in the actual box it's nice and safe and no one can get to it – like your feelings. Unless the moths come...

EMMA ON MISTY WATERCOLOUR MEMORIES

How to wander successfully down memory lane, from the one who found it too painful to think about

So, let's say you've gone through a loss. If you've read this many chapters of a book about it, that feels like a safe assumption. And let's say you went through your loss like I did, haplessly trying to chin-up and carry on, dragging the loss behind you in an iron box you've secured tightly with chains and ten padlocks to protect yourself against it. Well, there'll likely come a point in life when a little voice from inside the box starts calling out to you. And you might try to ignore it, but it keeps on talking, and then gradually the box will get closer and closer and closer until all you can hear is the voice, and the clank of the padlocks bashing on your ankles. And if that sounds like a terrifying nightmare, it's because that's how I felt about the memories attached to my own loss – terrified. Some people love to talk about and share the thing they lost, but when looking at what happened feels like a threat to your emotional stability, those thoughts themselves can become a threat, and memorializing feels pretty much impossible. While for Robyn that sharing felt warm and safe, for me it felt raw and dangerous – the ice burn you get after licking the freezer tray. And in fact, because you're so unaccustomed to accessing those emotions, it can feel like you're never going to get the tongue unstuck – as though you'll be permanently, painfully frozen in a space that renders you incapable of doing anything else.

That refusal to remember the loss itself or the good times that preceded it is the Emma Brain's expert self-preservation technique and it works really well if you want to spend your life with your fingers in your ears shouting "LA LA LA LA

LA LA LA!" at your mind. But, take it from somebody who's tried it both ways, however painful those memories are, being able to look at them is better than pretending they aren't there, and you're missing out on a whole lot of peace and happiness by denying them. Because when you can't allow yourself to think of the thing you lost, you're effectively taking a black paintbrush to the masterpiece that is your experience. And that can feel like the safest thing to do. Cover it up, numb it out, make it into a nothing. But there are ways to carefully restore that painting to greatness, uncovering the good bits, the characters, the individual brushstrokes, until you're able to stand back and look at the whole thing again, and appreciate it for what it was – a rich part of your life.

Scattered pictures
Of the smiles we left behind

If you went through your loss alone – by choice or by force – the chances are you won't have that community of people around you to naturally share your memories with. I get it. I'm an only child from my Mum and my Dad, am estranged from my step-dad, and live far away from Mum's other rellies and the friends she had in life. So the only person I really have to remember things with is me. It never really occurred to me that that was strange – and if you've lived your life doing all your emoting by yourself, it might feel totally normal to live a loss by yourself as well. You might actively seek out that aloneness because it means there are fewer places where the memories crop up, creating emotional and physical spaces that sweep the thing away and cushion you against it. For a long time that's how I lived, wilfully not looking at the thing because it hurt too much. If I'd have been part of Robyn's family of orators I'd have probably shrivelled into a prune and dried out in the corner gathering dust while they all got on with reliving the joy of her wonderful Nan. My family, on the other hand, aren't really big storytellers, and there's a lot of pain in our history, so I can understand why. I think everybody just preferred to look forwards and hope everything was going to be OK. Which is all a long-winded way of saying that how comfortable you feel memorializing the person or thing you lost is going to be roundly unique to you and yours, and if you come from a situation where sharing wasn't really on the menu, it might feel really alien and unsafe to call those things into focus, but with time and a bit of bravery on your part, it *is* possible. Maybe even enjoyable.

So, how do you do it? Gently. You might start by seeing if you can notice the things that make you want to run away and hide, because knowing what they are means you can create purposeful life-space to look at them, and mitigate some of the emotional bomb-shelling a surprise bit of contact can bring about. I'll give you an example: it took me years before I could listen to "You Got It" by Roy Orbison – the song my Mum and I used to sing in the car. When I was born, she had a pretty rough time of it with what I think we'd now call post-natal depression. Baby me cried and cried and wouldn't eat or sleep, and we struggled to bond, until one day she stood over my crib and looked at me and accidentally paraphrased Roy with, "Emma, whatever it takes – anything you want, anything you need – I'll do it." So that song always held particularly special significance for us both, and when she was alive we would listen to it in the car and sing it at each other and it was our shared thing and little secret experience. You might have a little nostalgic something like that attached to your loss – a smell, a joke, a landmark you see on the journey to an old workplace – and you'll know that experiencing that thing can put you right back in the place you were before the loss. Which, if you've been pretending the loss hasn't happened, is pretty heart-wrenching. So, for a long time I couldn't give Roy any airtime, but, with work and a little gently-gently, now I can, and when I hear it I know that I was cherished. And cherished in an imperfect way – the mother/daughter relationship that we see on the telly isn't always how it actually is. But there are ways to find the best in that, work through the difficulties and build something stronger than you might've had without the adversity. Just like loss. Yes, I got all that from Roy Orbison.

And how about actual, physical things? When I go to friends' houses, I'm always amazed at the walls of photos and memories they have on display – shrines to their own friends and families. It's lovely to see, and, if you're that way inclined, must feel so very wonderful and anchoring to have those people all around you. But in my little introvert space I need to disconnect from all that, so it's plain walls ahoy. And that goes for objects as well. I have a few things of my Mum's strewn about – the beautiful old walnut radio she had passed down when her own Father died, the giant stuffed hippo she sewed for me as a baby. For a while these things were hard to have around. Real tear-jerkers. But I think through having them nearby I've been able to sometimes get back to that place where the memories attached to them reside. Seeing the radio in my Mum's house, covered by a cloth in case it got marked, or me lying next to Hippo as a kid when he was the same size as me. Allowing myself to go back to those places has been a safe way to explore the memories and feel comfortable with them again. And that's the prize at the end of the tunnel of discomfort – you get to continue your relationship with the thing or person you lost, on your own terms. Sure, they might not be physically there with you, but the effects they had on your life live on, and that's the greatest memorial of all.

What's too painful to remember
We simply to choose to forget

If you're camped out at Lake Denial the sheer weight of all the memory waters trying to leak through your emotional tent doors might feel overwhelming, which probably makes you even less inclined to look at them. The longer you ignore them, the greater the weight and the higher the risk when you, say, read a letter from the person you lost. It can feel like if you stop bracing with all your might you'll drown in sadness for the rest of time, but the thing I didn't know in my loss, and that I want you to know, is that feeling those feelings isn't a permanent state. That it's safe to cross the lake to Sad Town and access that reservoir of feelings from wherever you are now. Drink at the watering hole, dip your toes in it, wallow in its shallow pools, because you won't get sucked under and you won't drown – behind the roaring waterfall of sadness is a whole bunch of wonderful memories.

I think sometimes we take loss Very Seriously Indeed, because often it is. But, in taking it Very Seriously, we can attach a lot of ceremony and organization to it, and become obsessed with finding the correct way of doing things. But memorializing a person or a thing or a moment in time doesn't need to be deadly serious. It can be messy, it can be funny – you don't need to order a floral arrangement and light candles in its honour. You don't even need to get dressed or stand up – all it takes is you and your mind getting together for a knees-up. Particularly with death-loss, there can be a sense of propriety and reverence about things that just might not speak to the way you're feeling. So you do you. Whatever you need to keep that memory going, do that. Where Robyn needs to be surrounded by people, I need space and time away from that to let my brain catch up with reality, and if you're somebody who's kept things in the emotional lockbox, you might need the same. That's OK, it's never too late to start on this journey. Sit by yourself, pick up an object – however you reconnect with your memories is completely up to you.

There's something about possessions attached to a loss that makes them oh-so precious, in a lock-them-up-when-clumsy-friends-come-over sort of a way. Indeed, there are a couple of things in my house that I have no sense of humour about. Like the unfathomable clay peacock bowl I made my Mum in Year 4 that's completely terrifying, but which she cherished, and that was in her hospital room when she died. I tense up when people are around it, and my partner knows that if anything happened to it there's a high chance he'd find parts of it inserted into parts of him. But – and this is something I'm still learning as I go – it's so important to remember that things are just things. They might help you to access a memory and they might feel wonderful to touch and have around you, but they are not what you lost. A prized ring is just metal and stone; a favourite teddy is just faux fur and stuffing; an award for great work is just brightly coloured Perspex – it's you that puts the meaning in them. The memories, the feelings, the thing that makes them special – that's all you. So I say try not to hold on too tightly. Sometimes we get so attached to looking after things that it becomes a kind of mania – we fear for them, and losing them feels like a disrespect – like losing the person or thing all over again. And there are some things, like letters or handmade items, that are precious, but if they're lost, everything attached to them still lives on. So let those things be a part of your life, not objects you have to live your life around. Wear the perfume, put on the ring, read the letters, display the frightening peacock bowl, because everything precious about them is already with you, and that can never be smashed by a careless hand or lost down the side of the sofa.

Then there are anniversaries. If your loss is related to a specific moment in time, these will pop around once a year to try and send you off at the deep end. I used to wonder why I felt so terrible for the entire month of October. With the help of a little therapy, I was able to understand that I was experiencing pre-Mumiversary bleurgh-ness – the state of mind that accompanies the anniversary of a big loss. Maybe you'll be inconsolable for weeks before, maybe it'll take you completely by surprise – I've experienced both. And if you recognize yourself in any of that, here's what I'd suggest: pop a note in your diary to recur every year. A gentle reminder that this bit is coming up, and you might need to be a little nicer to yourself. It doesn't need to say, "DIVORCE ANNIVERSARY IN THREE WEEKS." It could just say, "Book a massage" or "Be Kind To Yourself Month" – whatever reminder you need. Because anniversaries can hit hard – there's something about the time of year, perhaps, that your brain recognizes and remembers being traumatized around, and it calls into action all its best coping mechanisms. Only, as previously established, those mechanisms won't always work in your favour. And similarly, you might find the anniversary surprisingly easy to get through when you've

YOU **WILL** JUST

YOU **WILL** JUST

YOU **WILL** JUST

YOU **WILL** JUST

YOU **WILL** JUST

YOU **WILL** JUST

YOU **WILL** JUST

YOU **WILL** JUST

YOU **WILL** JUST

YOU **WILL** JUST

YOU **WILL** JUST

START TO *HEAL.*

START TO *HEAL.*

START TO *HEAL.*

START TO *HEAL.*

START TO *HEAL.*

START TO *HEAL.*

START TO *HEAL.*

START TO *HEAL.*

START TO *HEAL.*

START TO *HEAL.*

START TO *HEAL.*

been expecting much worse. Whatever happens, a little understanding can go a really long way. Making space to feel catatonically sad, having a contingency in case the sadness never comes – with just a little prep those days can loom less large.

My top anniversary tip is this: on the actual day, if there is one and if you're in a position to do it, give yourself the whole day to just be whatever you need. If you're anything like me, you'll want lots of alone time to feel whatever's there. It took me a long time to get to this point, but these days, on my Mumiversary, I take the full day, turn off my phone and isolate from the world. I'll watch her favourite film (*It's a Wonderful Life*), maybe look through some old photos and remember a time before my Mum was sick. I might write some stuff down, I'll definitely cry and I'll let my heart hurt for the woman I loved so hard and lost. If that sounds overwhelming, you could try starting a bit smaller – maybe add a little structure to the day, like: get up, have a bath, go for a walk, journal – and then be prepared to throw that structure out on the day if it's not what your heart wants you to do. Anniversaries of great losses are days to follow your instincts and give yourself whatever the heck you need. For Robyn, that's often a big cry and a nice distracting rollercoaster with friends; for me, it's (obviously) the opposite – the one day of the year I allow myself to completely indulge. And on that note, if you did go through a loss by yourself, having other people around who it doesn't affect can feel a bit wounding. They might unintentionally say something hurtful. Or behave in a way you'd rather they didn't. And if you know that you're somebody who guards their emotions fiercely, know also that it's OK to ask them for time alone. To tell them what you need, whether that's to make a big fuss or get the heck out of your hair. And try to let all the emotions happen, if you can. Cry, wail, lie in a heap on the floor, because all that emotion's in there already and it's going to find a way to come out, whether that's in authentic sadness or turn-it-on-yourself anxiety.

As an introvert, I'm always going to be about nailing down space and time to process things, but if your loss timeline is more amorphous and there isn't an exact date, you might feel like you're missing out on that chance to properly focus on it. You could try putting one in the diary – any day – so you know there's always a moment to process. Or you could try creating a thing or object that memorializes, so you know it's there when you need it. I have a scrapbook of little things I collected during the first throes of my career – wrist bands from Fashion Week, snatches of show write-ups, jokes my then-colleagues and I found hilarious. Sometimes looking through that book brings such a smile to my face – to see those things feels so transportative, and really highlights the journey I've been on since, to get to where I am. Because loss – any loss – is a journey, and it's down to you to find your own path through it.

So it's the laughter
We will remember
Whenever we remember
The way we were

My Mum's still with me. I talk to her now and then – I tell her I love her. And I take both comfort and pain in having found a path that I know she'd be proud of. One of my saddest things in having lost my Mum so young is that she never got to see who I became. But I know that she'd have been into it. And she'd love those moments when I'm able to sit with her for a bit, too. Remembering and paying tribute to somebody or something you lost can be an emotional access point, a chance for connection, and a moment to understand how your relationship with that person or thing is progressing. Because it will change over time, and that's OK – good, even. Nothing in this life stands still, and there's no reason your grief will either. Allowing your relationship with it to grow and mature and morph can be life-changing if you let it.

ACTION STATIONS
How to do a little remembrance when it's
all a bit much.

- Start small. Try to notice if your brain gets
  a bit flustered when a particular memory floats
  into view. Maybe write it down so you can look
  at it later.

- Think of an object attached to the thing you lost
  and write down a matter-of-fact description of
  what it looks like. Then expand that to describe
  the setting you remember it in. Then again to
  describe what you're doing in that memory. If
  any emotions come up, note those down too.
  Sometimes seeing the object as just an object can
  help us feel safe enough to access the feelings
  attached to it.

- Close your eyes. Think of one happy memory
  with the thing you lost – a time you were smiling
  or laughing. Let yourself feel whatever comes up.

ROBYN ON MISTY
WATERCOLOUR MEMORIES

Ways to memorialize things from someone who sees
life as a mobile museum of self

I have an absolute leg-up on memorializing because it's very
much a family tradition, on my wild, uncensored Sephton
side and on my slightly Victorian, don't-misbehave-please
Donaldson side. Both are fiercely proud of where they come
from and we talk about relatives living, and mainly dead, all
the time. I feel I know people I never met, or not in a sentient
way, intimately. They are folklore. Their story is my story.
There are countless pictures of them about. I know all about
my Nanny Nin, who died well before I was born. About my
grandad's brother who ran over the psychic.[1] That I am
related to the, famously, "biggest woman in Ormskirk" who
had to be hoisted out of her, I think, canal boat when she
died and that my great Granny[2] Joe had not one but two
chameleons in the war. I also know how he was nearly killed,
a lot, and that he seldom spoke about that chapter of his life.
I know that my super awesome great, great Auntie Eve was
one of the first women to own a motorbike in the UK and
had a big silver dish she made displayed in the (second) Great
Exhibition, or something like that, because actually no-one
in my family can actually remember what it was. It's all really
bloody nice. To feel part of a historical tradition of renegades
and to be rooted somewhere. I feel honoured to have been
brought up to feel so proud of where I come from, even the
shit bits.

---

1   I honestly am not making that up.
2   Like most children, I couldn't pronounce shit and had real issues with
grandad. So my great-grandad was Granny Joe and my grandad is Buddy
'cos he was my buddy. Obviously.

My Nan's house is very much ground zero for my memory hoarding tendencies – there are photo albums and gallery walls and pieces of jewellery and bits of furniture and war medals and tea sets, and the vast majority comes from our family. They become visual prompts, spinning out from the original tale to endless stories about whoever was mentioned, their uncle, his mistress, the milkman, who, if you're wondering, ran off to Spain with all the milk money. It's like having an innate set of museum reference plaques. I love hearing them and I love telling them. So when Nan died, I was ready to preserve her immediately like some lunatic emotional embalmer. I wanted to gather everything I could and place it around me like a magpie, safe in my shiny little nest of memories. I wore her clothes, her jewellery, her shoes. Luckily, I was in her house so I was quite literally swaddled in her stuff. I got a tattoo for her about three days after she died (as did my brother), despite being told under no uncertain terms not to. Though I'm pretty sure she knew we'd do it anyway. I became fixated on physically keeping her around. Her texts on my phone, the sound of her voice in my head, the smell of her, how she seemed to turn up the heating ten degrees when she walked into a room because she was just that kind of comfort. I compulsively archived because then maybe I could create a version of her. Enough to fill the Nan-shaped hole.

Not so, unfortunately. Because as I've said before, I always have the following response in a time of loss:

1. Get mad (anger)
2. Freak out (fear)
3. Distract myself and try to change something (control)
4. Fall on the floor crying (sadness)

Which is impossible if you actually lost it in the forever sense. I do it with clothes, letters, the colour of my hair as it greys, even the dog, who I have considered cloning. I absolutely did it with Nan. It's a very intense, manic period based on a fragile delusion and the need to be doing something. It just ended up making me sadder and very anxious I'd lose one of the many things I was traipsing around with. Like the guy who walked through our village with a wheelbarrow of stuff when I was a child and who I was scared shitless of. Anyway, the point is, I've never really had success with the pseudo-Frankenstein method. It's also a sure-fire route to becoming a hoarder, so instead I'm trying to focus on healthy, realistic ways of memorializing someone, or something, which I will handily lay out here in the hope it helps you too.

Keep talking

I love Emma. I have been incredibly grateful that someone as uniquely kind, calm and emotionally intuitive as her has been my primary companion on my biggest loss expedition. I could not have done it without her. She's taught me to look at things in different, less frantic ways and has been a tremendous comfort, in an odd sibling/parent/pal style. But in retrospect, one thing I should have devoted more time to was corralling Emma into talking about her Mum. Because I was talking about my Nan all the damn time. I didn't even know Emma's Mum's name until fairly recently. Berenice, if it slipped your mind. I didn't know Emma hadn't lived with her from being quite so young or just how tough her Mum had it. Because, as second nature as my need to discuss things with people is, I didn't want to scare the horses.

Imagine you've got an incredibly, easy-to-spook nervous horse. Let's, for argument's sake, call it Emma. What you mustn't do is go up to it and throw your arms around it and say "I love you. You're mine now. Don't be worried", because that will really worry Emma (the horse). You have to stand at a distance, whistling, with something nice in your hand. For many hours. After months of tiny advancements, Emma the horse might make it up to your hand, take a tiny nibble and then career away and you have to start the whole delicate process again. Now I didn't go and grab Emma (not the horse). But I also didn't bring her an incentivizing treat. I stood at the other end of the field shouting "Dude, are you OK?" and she'd be like "Yeah, absolutely fine", and I'd think "Well, I can't push her so fine it is." What I should have done is ask questions. And not stop. In a soft way. I know my bud well enough to know she'll give me a "No, thank you" if she doesn't want to discuss things but equally, I could have been more leading. Let her tell me her story. Make it feel more natural and less horrifying or just not a big deal. With all her losses, 'cos lord knows, she's had a few, I wish I'd just said, "If you can, tell me more about that feeling. Or moment. Or person." Because people like Emma don't feel like people want to hear their story so they don't tell them. Whereas people like me think everyone wants to know as it's such a jolly good tale. I commit on paper to ask more, my lovely friend.

Because talking, above anything, is the single most effective way of keeping someone's memory alive and to add to the picture you already had of them. Less so with things but with situations or periods of time or people, having a natter about it can be really helpful. Others will add dimensions to the picture you see that you never considered or reinforce what you already knew. Some conversations will be very difficult, like talking about a child you lost or sibling

LIKE A MAGPIE I WANTED TO GATHER EVERYTHING AND PLACE IT AROUND ME or spouse. But you illuminate them when they come into conversation, I'm sure. They become more 4D and you see the colour of their hair was slightly different in someone else's mind or re-feel the tininess of their hand or tick, tick, tick of their heartbeat. You'll see things from camera two instead of camera one and to have more to look at when your viewing experience was painfully cut short can be a blessing. Albeit a devastatingly bittersweet one. I hope there's comfort in adding to that memory bank.

With more straightforward, linear losses these alternative views are more easily absorbed and framed as just glorious reaffirmation. I have heard stories of my Nana's kindness that confirm I have her absolutely right. And to know that she was basically universally seen how I saw her makes me giddy and very proud.

Even talking to people very close to you, your views will be fortified, but they also add some bonus material, like a director's cut where you learn a little extra about the person or situation. It can work to enhance the scenes you play in your mind, vindicate you for walking away from something or just act as a bloopers reel.

For me, there's just a cacophony of joy when I speak about people that aren't around anymore, especially with my raucous Northern family. Like those shows you see on Victoria Wood or George Michael where people confirm they were as excellent as you thought and then some. That they had hidden depths you hadn't even anticipated. I am blanketed in those moments, which are primarily filled with laughter, and for a second my Nan or my Granny or my crotchety Auntie Mary are just off stage, tantalizingly close. I love it when we come together and celebrate them. Because we also cement ourselves back together and re-experience the closeness we had when they were there and everything was just a little less shit. So I implore you, find a way to talk about lost things, and then they're gone but not forgotten.

Museum of self

OK, there is something about having a museum of self that screams, "I am a psychopath." But I'm not, I promise. A narcissist certainly, but I don't believe I pose a current threat to the public. I do believe that any space we occupy for a meaningful amount of time should reflect us and what we need back. That we should imbue it with a sense of our story – the one we've had and the one we want. That we should be surrounded by things that say something. Not just, "I got this in Ikea", but, "This is who I am, and where I came from, and what inspires me, and where I hope to end up." I know that's very much an all-in approach, but for extroverts big memory placards tend to work a treat. It might sound indulgent, but don't forget it's something we seemed much better at a few decades ago, with our display cabinets and portraits and more deeply personal things all out on show. When we didn't have soap operas or Netflix boxsets, our heritage was part of the entertainment.

It can be tough to work out how to bring that sense of memorialization into the home without setting up a 12ft shrine, replete with candles. And if a shrine is your vibe, go for it. But there are ways of memorializing things in a passive, low-key way as well as a "Whack-out-the-trumpets – I loved my time at Trumpet School" fashion. You can display things attached to a person or period of time and by singling them out and giving them a purposeful home they are elevated. Tickets or postcards or old corks popped in happier times. You can have a memory box if they're just for you or a ruddy great shelf if you want to open things up for examination. These historical artefacts are a quick journey to the moments you want to keep hold of, so treasure them... though not too much, they aren't the memory itself. Or if that's too hard, you can nod to them. Create little tributes. Things that are beautiful and meaningful, so you have the option of divulging why they're so beloved. I have a gilded sign of a phrase my Nan used, a print of the weird thing I muttered after first snogging my husband, a tattoo that is just a lovely moon but contains a cloud from an Arthur Rackham illustration my dad got me. Turning your memories into accessible art is kind of a millennial form of historical portraiture. You create beauty from something taken away. You can have it around you always. There's a comfort in that.

So whether you keep a drawer full of business cards from your first job, endless photos of uni high jinks with people who have faded away or a page containing the inked footprints of a baby born asleep, consider bringing those memories into your everyday. That way they're normalized to the point they aren't a terrible surprise and put on the pedestal they deserve, because those memories and access to them can be the most precious thing in the world.

Getting your ass down to memory lane

I've said it before and I'll say it again, there are ways to fast-track emotions, and I am so here for that. There are things that take me immediately back to a time and place and sometimes that's lovely. Not if you're crying in the fish aisle while doing your Asda big shop but in the privacy and safety of your own home, it can be glorious. For me, music is a really important access point to memories as it transports you right back to a moment in time or a person or a scenario or place. Formalizing that to use as a handy memory aid is as simple as setting up a Spotify playlist.

It can prompt a grateful, grinning walk as you listen to a megamix of songs inspired by old lovers. It can be wailing to "Coat of Many Colors" and knowing how lucky you were to be so loved by someone, just like Dolly was. It can be the nerve-zapping euphoria of hearing the opening chords of "Set You Free" by N-Trance and remembering the heady feeling of possibility that comes from being part of a group of underage girls off for a night out in Liverpool. And for a time how great a half-tablet of ecstasy was. How your life was going to be incredible with no complications and you were just pure, distilled optimism. And how much you absolutely never want to do ecstasy again. It's being about four and feeling so grown up sat in the crook of your dad's arm watching a Bob Marley concert 'cos you couldn't sleep or screaming The Pogues at the top of your voice with your Mum on a weird trip to Wales. It's a powerful thing. But you have to go looking. Keep reminding yourself that actively looking for memories is worth it. There's gold in them there hills, but you need to leave the house (or at least switch on your nearest device) to mine it. It could be visiting a park you used to go to, going and getting ice cream somewhere you went as a child or even (and this does NOTHING for me) popping in for a graveyard visit. Being an active participant in the scavenger hunt that is looking back is pretty bloody essential, and the rewards are well worth it.

Now ignore everything I just said...

The most useful thing I realized is that the most important bits of my Nan, and everyone and everything I've loved and that have gone away, live inside of me. Microscopic. Like micro plastics. You can't consume them without absorbing bits into yourself. And those bits float in your bloodstream, informing everything. Everything I do is down to innumerable influences that pull me this way and that before I settle on a course of action. In the good choices I make and the things I am proud of I feel my Nan completely. She's there driving me with a little joystick. Look at the thing you lost and know that the unbearable nature of it not being around anymore is exactly why the fragments of it are not going anywhere. It's peppered through the marrow of your bones. Nice, albeit a bit gross. Even if the loss you experienced was welcome – the fact that you feel its loss means that, in there, somewhere, is something to be figured out, learnt from or put to bed. So even though it's uninvited, know it lingers 'cos it can offer you something – perhaps that's to steer you away from the harmful stuff.

To give a very obvious illustration of what I mean about them being stored in your DNA, I have to confess something: I think I've lost my Nana's emails. All of them. Except one. Time was when that would have been the end of the actual world. I would have been inconsolable. But when I look at that solitary email now I'm not saddened that I can't look at more. I'm reassured that I know her voice so well that I could have written it. That she sits there as part of my subconscious. That she's less of a person and more of a language I speak, secretly, to other people who knew her. She is the Barbara Theory and although she's not around to tell me how to do things, sometimes in ways I did not agree with, she slipped a compass into my hand when she left. And it leads me back to her and forwards to the life I know she'd have taken so much joy in. That email, if boiled down, just says one thing over and over again and that is "You are adored." To have that is a remarkable thing, and one that can't just be snuffed out when the sender is taken away.

So now, though things are still completely beloved, I'm learning to look at the sum *and* the parts and appreciate that the reason a loss is so difficult is centred around the fear of losing the invisible stuff. I'm discovering that the wonderful, intangible things aren't going anywhere so I needn't rush to create a Frankenstein's monster from all the bits and bobs that made something great. Keep and adore things, sure, but equal celebration of the seen and unseen stuff makes for a good balance, I reckon. And that is all I have to say on that.

ACTION STATIONS
Memorializing without being creepy.

- Scrap books are good. I think they need to make a comeback. Great for all the faff you treasure like gig tickets and photos and little notes and stuff you want to keep just for you.

- Get artistic. Think about how you want to memorialize something and how to make that really beautiful. Blow up an old photo, have an art print of a favourite saying or a map of special journeys. There are so many ways of repackaging memories and making them a permanent part of your surroundings.

- Celebrate the treasure. Make new traditions involving those things so you have an excuse to have them out on occasion. Grandma's sherry glasses for Emma. My Nan's tea set for me. .... for you.

Dr Sheetal Says...

How do we think about the lost thing safely? The final stage of grief is usually acceptance. This is when we have come to terms with the fact that what we have lost is actually lost and that the best way to move on from it is to acknowledge this and live alongside the memory. This might be the first time you start to relive those moments with the lost person or thing and that it feels OK. Yes, life might be different, but there is hope for it to still be meaningful.

The reason that you are suffering greatly is probably because that person or thing made your life amazing in so many ways, so it does not make sense to write them or it out of your life forever. When the time comes, those memories will be enriching and beautiful. Getting your feelings out there is SO important. That could be by talking and describing your loss to others – from here you will gain perspective in addition to that feeling of getting stuff off your chest. You may even hear about other losses, which may reassure and soothe you. If it was the loss of a person, bring them to life with memories. Remember why you are missing them so much. It's highly likely that it's because you adored that person and how they cherished you and made you feel about yourself. So remind yourself of that, because those are the qualities you want to keep in your life. Having reminders around you (or even on you) can be comforting, but overindulging or obsessing over someone or something and keeping their possessions all around you is less healthy and potentially further traumatizing. Focus on the good memories in good proportions and remind yourself of what that person or thing brought into your life and how it impacts on the way you live now. The material things will be there (and some day they might not be) but those memories, the intricacies of the way you are, is what lives on and is most important.

Not now but soon

With enough time _____

With enough distance _____

Waiting for the kettle, suddenly _____

Understanding the unfathomable _____

_____ it will be like it never happened

_____our bodies will forget

_____ we'll be drawn backwards

_____ things the other said

"Of course we know, we have absorbed the
knowledge deeply into our bodies, deeper, into
our cells, we have offered and received the cliche
countless times in earnest tones: it will get easier.
But knowing that doesn't make loss any more
bearable. The entire collection this poem is from,
and this poem in particular, is a manifestation of
that sentiment; that this suffering, like all else, will
eventually become a memory. And in fact, soon
enough, it will be impossible to feel it in the way
you feel it now. I ask myself once I've finished a
thing, what is this for? Is it useful? And I figured
this collection could be useful if only it could offer
that; a real time detailing of exactly that thing.
That no matter how it feels right now, if you can
bear it, you will bear it. "

Poet and recording artist Kae Tempest on the
ways loss becomes a part of you, written in
response to their poem *Not Now But Soon*

YOU 2.0

When nothing feels like it will ever be the same again, how can loss begin to feel like a force for good in your life?

Emma: So this is it. The grand moment. Phoenix from the flames.

Robyn: Still a very sad phoenix, just crucially not ON fire.

Emma: I don't think the sadness really ever goes away.

Robyn: No, but it is less regular... sometimes just as potent though.

Emma: We both felt guilty for having the thing that losing them gave us, and I think it's taken me a while to get used to the fact that it's OK to build on your loss foundations.

Robyn: It is very difficult to sit with the fact you did some good shit because a Very Bad Thing happened. Not in spite of it – literally because of it. I know I would not want to change those years, but equally it would be great if Nan wasn't dead.

Emma: Yeah, if my Mum hadn't died, I would not be doing a lot of the things that I am doing. And I wouldn't know myself as well as I do. Those losses took so much away from us, but allowed us to have so much in return.

ROBYN ON YOU 2.0

What comes after loss, from the one who can't bear a story without a moral

Ok, strap in for some sweeping statements, controversial hypotheses and a smattering of conflicting information because this chapter is going to be an absolute doozy. I'll start with the big one: I believe my loss freed me. Which is a very difficult thing to acknowledge as it also popped me into an eternal glass box of emotion. But that box was handily magnified, and it set a lot of the problems I thought I had into relief, against the backdrop of one big unsolvable one. Not that I'd rather have that than the things that went away. But I wouldn't go back. But it helped me move forward. But I would give anything to have my Nan here. But I wouldn't want to be the Robyn I was when she was. And therein lies the terrible contradiction of loss: both helpful and an absolute hinderance.

Losing something is always accompanied by a massive dose of associated learning. Even if that learning is as simple as "I hated to lose that thing." When and only when you're with it enough to properly assess what's going on around you, you'll look up at the path ahead and realize you're actually at the start of the *Gladiator* assault course, or *The Floor Is Lava*. Someone blows a whistle and you're left looking forward to something that is completely farcical in its impossibility. You are tired, you already did all the challenges before when everything was a blur and now someone is expecting you to have the superhuman strength it requires to jump, lift, sprint and dangle your way to emotional freedom. Plus, there's not even a trophy at the other end, just another slightly easier assault course. And then an easier one again. And so on until getting around

Loss freed me but also

popped me

of emotion.

into an eternal glass box

your loss takes all the energy of bossing a children's activity playground. It took a lot to get there. You have terrible shin splints and giant blisters. You cried with agony tonnes. But now you can do it with relative ease.

If you told me when I first lost anything, even my favourite scarf[1], that I'd be changed, and perhaps in some ways improved, by learning to live without that thing, I would to this day probably thump you in the guts. But in the fullness of time, I'd calm down, have a big think and acknowledge that accepting the unknowingness of life and the fragility of relationships, with people, places and things is pretty OK. That the narrative we create for ourselves that we hold on to so fiercely, and that serves as our internal compass, leading us on towards a fate we consider predestined, is, in reality, completely beyond the realms of our control. That the script we write for our lives changes daily, mainly in imperceptible ways, and sometimes in massive, hideous ones that incinerate all the pages. We are always adjusting the focus, re-tuning our fuzzy TV sets and leaning into the plot twists. We don't tend to notice the colleague leaving, the way our bodies change over the course of a year, the wearing out of clothes or the newsagents turning into a coffee shop. But we do notice the brakes-on, about-turn end of a romance, the death of a friend, the conclusion of a career or an irreversible change to our health or circumstances. And we just do a bigger pivot. The direction we are heading in is adjusted and us with it.

And that next-generation us, heading south-south-east

---

1 Formative memory of university being very, very drunk and making all my friends search for my Nana's rainbow scarf that I lost at some kind of outdoor freshers piss up. Miraculously, they did find it.

instead of just south-east, will learn new things, by osmosis and by the loss itself. It's multi-layered and passive and inevitable. Which is nice when everything seems such a terrible, burdensome effort. Losing Barbara came with bonus serving of profound enlightenment, which was convenient. That was the almost immediate realization that my Nan had actually been all the things I'd so desperately wanted my Mum to be. She had been caring and nurturing and challenging and just a joy. I loved being around her. When I was, I felt at home and protected. My sanctuary. Not perfect by any means, who is, but just always there. And then she wasn't and suddenly I realized I'd been *wanting* so hard I didn't enjoy the *having* enough. That I had an extraordinary relationship with Nan and with the teachers I've mentioned and friends, and friend's mums, and relatives of all descriptions, and the various other people that had dropped into my life at just the right time to scoop me up. That I had received more love than your average. And suddenly instead of feeling like the unlovable daughter I felt tremendously lucky. What a thing to be loved in abundance.[2] Surely with that in your back pocket you can do anything. All you need really *is* love.

Lose it

For the first few weeks, months or years (depending on your timeline) after losing something, what fills the space that the lost thing filled is a sense of loss for that thing. Like a security blanket knitted out of memories, you just wrap that round you and are comforted by the facsimile of the actual thing. That's OK for a bit. In early loss you deserve that relief and I say relish walking around in your blankie like a toddler. But

2 I won't say I am the people's princess but am I the people's princess?

there comes a time where you have to pull off the comforter and take stock. Hideous I know but actually, the blanket is getting a bit ripe and you need to let your skin breathe. That's when it's time to look at loss.

Examining it can be hard, because you can't detach the loss from the self. Maybe imagine putting everything in your life on a very long shelf. Just all of it. Turn every precious thing into a china figurine. One day, the world is going to just straight up knock that shelf down. GULP. And shock horror, one thing is not going to make it. But let's not focus on the lost thing cos you've had ages to do that. Let's look at everything on the floor. It's a mess but luckily the rest is intact. And you'll check on the things in order of priority. You will rank things in terms of importance. Notice that if you can. Which things you are quickest to pick up and give you the most comfort. Where you put them back on the shelf. What takes centre stage and which things gently fill the gaps of your favourite thing now smashed to smithereens. In the moments you are least able to rifle through your feelings, what you do on autopilot will be very revealing. Autopilot me didn't reach for my Mum, in fact, she saw that my Mum was a life-sized porcelain poodle and was taking up a lot of room on the shelf, obscuring the view of the other treasured things and actually being a bit of a liability. That sounds really cold and really harsh but that space she was taking up was wasted because of the nature of the relationship. So I took her off the shelf. I wouldn't have been able to if I still had my Nan on the shelf as they were a matching set and the Nan figurine was, handily, also installed with a speaker and would regularly say, "Robyn, all I want is for you and your mum to get along." And because I loved Nan very much it was easier to relent. I saw my relationship with my

Mum completely differently PBD[3] so she stayed on the shelf taking up so much bloody room. But ABD[4] I had the freedom to choose. All the wonderful expectations I wanted to live up to were gone but so were the things I did out of duty. I think that's why some families completely implode when they lose someone. Because the silent obligations and standards they had to live up to are gone and everyone loosens their waistbands and breathes out and admits they didn't actually like Uncle Carlos after all. Don't get me wrong, some knit together even tighter and that is glorious. But some, like mine, don't.

It's like leaving a job – sometimes you think you've got the best damn group of colleagues in the world, that you will be in touch with Dakshi, Claudia and Frank forever. Two years down the line you're actively avoiding them on Facebook. It was circumstance that made it feel great, not the line-up. But sometimes you worked with a fantastic group of cats and five years later you still have a thoroughly entertaining WhatsApp group, a small business and are real friends because the universe knew you were better together. The result of a loss is only knowable in the past tense. But my main point is that, in losing something, you may allow yourself to shed other things that don't serve you – because of lack of obligation or because with a new perspective you see it's not right for you or, just reduced capacity. That's good and healthy and removes some unnecessary emotional heft from your already spilling-over knapsack of everything.

---

3 Pre-Barbara Dying.
4 After Barbara Dying (I wanted this to be Post Barbara Dying but you can see the problem with that by glancing at the last footnote).

Use it

I never thought I'd use Kim Kardashian as a poster girl for anything, ever. But when I say you can gather up all the things you learned through loss, pop them in a blender and sprinkle in a touch of please-be-proud-of-me-[insert name] and a splash of I-can-do-anything-if-I-just-did-that then you'll create a nourishing smoothie guaranteed to power you on to get though the day, I mean it. What has this got to do with the Kardashians, I hear you cry? Well, I'll tell you. Kim Kardashian is a woman who very publicly lost a parent, relationships, the shape of the family that came next, friendships and one copy of a sex tape. I spent a long time thinking, "Ewwww Kim K, seriously, give it a rest. I've seen more of your naked body than conceivably my own," but now I say "Kimmy, I hear your sonar – you're a woman treading a weirdly similar path to me and I've time for that." Because Kim Kardashian lost a dad who seemed like her everything, and now she's doing one of the most empowering things you can do with that loss. She's honouring it. Not with SKIMS or her lovely highlighters but by being inspired by and energized through her dad's memory. She's using his faith in her to try to become an actual lawyer. Who saw that coming? But it's cool. I get it. I look at Kim Kardashian and I think, "You're a bit amazing, to do that. To use his love for something excellent. To say, 'This is what he gave me and I'll be damned if I waste it whatever the entire global population thinks.'" What a tribute. Much better than the appalling hologram Kanye gave you for your birthday...

Losing someone doesn't mean losing the sense of who they thought you were or the fact they fervently believed you could do anything. My Nan honestly said to me, regularly and from me being a tiny dot, "You can be anything you want to be, even the Prime Minister." Now I think she might have been a little misguided, but that confidence bolstered me. It pushed me forward and made me feel entitled to be in certain rooms, confident that my voice should be heard, and that I was special and unique and gifted. That's the minimum any parent should instil – the sense that their child is extraordinary. Robert Kardashian gave that to his children and it's still there. His voice in their subconscious, egging them on – telling them they can be anything. It's unmissable and when you look at them through that lens, pretty excellent. You might not share their aspirations but to see a family who are so informed by someone who's gone, who feel invincible because a person had the ultimate faith in them – well that's inspiring. They used that to literally take over the world.

And the lost thing doesn't have to be as momentous as a parent – it could be a job that made you feel capable, a lover who made you feel lovable, a nervous dog that taught you that you just have to be infinitely patient. Let the traces of them fuel you, help you know yourself better and form the current version of You 2.0. They're written into your coding now and will hopefully make you softer and more self-aware – like Arnie in *Terminator 2*.

I used Nan's faith in me to push myself forward and I used the situation that loss left me in to do something I'd always wanted to. I have always written. Always. But it took my Nan dying to find something big enough to write about in a prolonged way. It started with the notebook I kept to give to her after she got better charting all the humorous things that happened while she was sick. It ended with this, totally different book that you're reading right now. It made me look at what I wanted to be and also what I wanted to put out into the world. What I want to be is helpful. If just one person reads this and feels a little less hopeless then I will have done her proud. She taught me the importance of caring, she meted it out liberally, and while I won't be the matriarch of the kind of massive, unruly family she was so proud of, I'll use her teachings in my own style. I'll do care my way. Because this book is mainly there to say I'm here and I see you and although I don't know you, I care. About you and whatever hideous predicament you find yourself in. By gosh, there's a value to that. As I've said, probably too much, the importance of feeling understood cannot be understated.

So use all of it. Lay out all the things that you're left with after loss, all the things that you like and don't. All the things that have changed and the ways you are rebuilt and the new expertise you've acquired. Do a skills audit on you. Sounds demented but look at you now. The you that survived. The resourceful, powerful, unsinkable you. And think about all the things you have and how you could use them. How they could create a toolkit to make you happier, the spaces that are left to fill and the new freedoms you're now afforded. Write it down if it's helpful, think of it like that weird career test you did in secondary school – it's likely the results will be quite different now from the ones you got at 16. It will help you see a new path when everything is a bit smoggy. And who doesn't love a big shouty road sign.

Improve it

Now this is the one that will have people rolling their eyes. Let's go next-level. You've pruned back the things that no longer fits in the new world you inhabit, you've looked at the fragments of what's left and the map they form going forward, now you have to look at how YOU fit into this and do some of that hacking back and building up on yourself. Because YOU can also actively shape You 2.0. You can be brutal. You can be courageous. You can be very honest. You can say, "I have to work on me to be the me I want to be." Once again for anyone in the back row: THERAPY. Think of who and what you want to be and what you, in isolation, have to do to achieve that. It's very easy to think you've gone through a lot and aren't you an absolute hero for making it, and dude, you are. But you are also a human being which means you are deeply flawed. You may have been forced to grow in ways that aren't helpful but that's (not so easily) remedied. The natural shape of me is self-involved, impatient, and cruel if provoked. Loss made me want to be better at this. There was a shift towards it because of circumstances of course, but it also takes active work. So, look at the ways you came out of this – you're probably a bit bent out of shape but you can work out a strategy for putting that right. Muddle out how you can be the very best You 2.0 you can imagine. It might be talking or journaling or having tough conversations. Having a look at how you can actively improve you is not an easy step; it will be uncomfortable and infuriating and take effort but it's a step that will make you disproportionately happier in the long run.

So there you have it, some ways that loss can benefit you. How becoming familiar with its shape and form can make its learnings transferable to all different kinds of loss and, in that way, take the edge off them too. As my grandad says it's "better for knowing" and it really is. It is less scary and more of an unfortunate inevitability. To be forewarned is to be forearmed and I really think as a society we don't give loss anywhere near enough airtime. It might make you bold enough to start the business you always dreamed of. It might make you calm enough to no longer see the world's problems as your problems because you have encountered the biggest and most unsolvable problem there is. It might not seem to change you at all. I can't say the pros outweigh the cons and I bounce between gratitude for the person my experiences have allowed me to become and the fury for the huge hole I still have inside. It's a process but if you take one thing from this chapter, let it be to know that it *might* not be all bad.

ACTION STATIONS
How to get the best out of You 2.0.

- Sit down and make a list comparing old you and new you. Like that bad list Ross makes about Rachel in *Friends*. Get to know the bits of new you that trump your past self and have a think about how you can use them.

- Ask a pal. It can be hard to pinpoint the ways you're different but a friend will sure as hell have noticed.

- Try not to feel guilty. You shouldn't feel bad that you had to adapt to a situation that was terrible and that, in turn, improved you. Speak to peers about it. The chances are a lot of them will feel the same.

EMMA ON YOU 2.0

What comes after loss, from the one who thought it would be bad forever

Back over in Introvert's Corner and I'm thinking about how much longer it took me than Robyn to figure out the positives in loss. There wasn't a moment or a thing that suddenly fell into place like her understanding of her relationship with her Mum, but for me it's been a slow graduation into a place that feels better than it used to.

The paradox of loss is that by losing something, you often *gain* something else. Not just the ability to cry for days on end – you might also get to open up the doorway to different parts of yourself. Steered into a different way of being; forced to balance on one stilt instead of two, you'll learn so much about yourself, and get to understand yourself better in this bold new world. The inclination might be to hang on for dear life to what was there before – in the choppy seas of loss, letting go of the life raft of familiarity can feel like the most dangerous thing you can do, because of course, you think you'll sink. But imagine letting go and finding out you not only float, but discover you can swim. The all-inclusive cruise ship you were on might have been wrecked and sunk to the bottom of the ocean, but you're not adrift – far from it – in fact, you're going to swim yourself to shore on some tropical island you've never heard of, and build a life for yourself there, full of richness and bounty. And on the island you'll find other people who've survived that same choppy sea, and you'll help each other find shelter and safety.

For the people who get to that point, loss is never final – it's a new beginning and can help to lay the foundations of a stronger you. It's like being chucked into a pit of slow-moving quicksand – you have to get out, or you'll perish, and on the way out you'll develop some killer biceps you can then use to do lots of heavy-lifting back in real life. It's about moving towards the things that scare you the most, and getting comfortable in their presence. There's rarely a shortcut to get to the good stuff, but if you can put in the work, whether that's hand-embroidering your own mourning shroud, sitting very still with your sadness, or seeking out that external help, there's contentment and peace to be found on the other side.

If you're newly in your loss, this might all feel a bit much. I know when my Mum died that finding anything other than the completely-terrible in it would've felt like a betrayal. So, if that's you, treat this like it's a hazy, imagined story – something you might want to think of a little further down the line. Because there's no rush. Nobody's saying you need to get there now. But to know that it won't be Bad Times forever – that's the thing.

Initiating download

This might be uncomfortable to read, but I am glad every day that I went through my Big Loss. I will never be glad that my Mum is dead, and I still feel pain for her in my heart, but I'm thankful for everything I've learned from the experience of living through losing her. When I think of the person I was before, I was so lost, so afraid, so ungrounded in the world and unsure of my own self. And without having lived through the worst possible thing, I might never have needed to break out of that cycle – that normal. Losing my Mum was hell, and I lived through some truly traumatic moments because of it, but from the other side I can see that it made me face up to what was bad in my life. Made me look at something *so* bad I couldn't use my traditional coping mechanisms and bury it. And I know myself better than I ever would've done without having lost my Mum. When life kicks your emotional crutches out from under you, you find out whether you can stand. And it sometimes shows you that one of the legs you're standing on is broken. You might try for a really long time to stand on it, but it just keeps getting broken in more and more places, until eventually you have to sit down and let it heal. Sure, the healing's painful and takes a long time, but it's also nourishing and leaves you stronger and more unshakeable. And your healing journey will be all your own – each one different to the last. Where Robyn wanted to re-market her loss as partially positive from early on, I would never have been able to do that. Wouldn't have wanted to if I could. I was living Brand Doom. I thought for a long time that that's just what life was like after you lost your best person – just really rubbish all the time. But it's not. It gets better. With work and time and a lot of kindness to yourself it does get better.

We might want to look at loss as a blip to be processed and moved on from, but that removes the genuine goodness from the situation. Loss never really goes away – it feeds into all the other bits of life if you let it, in the very best ways. The understanding you have of yourself, the compassion you feel for others – it's all on the loss buffet table and you can help yourself. Heck, you can go fetch a plate of it for other people if you like – there's plenty to go around.

Grow your roots
I often think of change – any change – like repotting a plant (you're the plant in this analogy). It's probably relatively comfortable in the pot, but a little cramped and your roots are getting kind of tangled and you know you're not going

to be able to flower very much unless you get a new pot. Only getting to the new pot requires vulnerability. There'll be a moment where your precious roots are on show, all white and gnarly, and you have to shake all the soil off them and they'll feel exposed. And then you get into the bigger pot and it still feels a bit shocking to be there, but gradually, slowly, you bed in and stretch out and before you know it, that new pot is home and you're growing new shoots and flowering like Elton John's garden. The process of any change is uncomfortable, but change so often brings about something good. So imagine what good a monumental, life-altering change like loss could bring about. Yes, loss is shit, but shit is fertilizer and fertilizer makes things grow.

The other thing about loss is that it is unavoidable, unless you actually do go and live in a hut by yourself forever. Because loss of a thing is the counterbalance to having a thing – you can't experience one without having had the other. If you have something, one day, unless you and that thing live forever, it will go away. I don't know how comforting that is, but I think I find a little solace in knowing that the vast sadness I've had for my Mum came about because of the vast love we shared when she was alive. That the feeling of aloneness I've felt exists because I had oneness with her. It reminds me that there was good before there was bad. And I think that's quite a nice thing. One of the less-good things my loss gave me is a hypervigilance for signs of future loss. So I worry when somebody doesn't message back that they hate me and have left for good; I used to panic when my partner left the house in case he got hit by a bus – you get the idea. It's fun in my head. But the thing I also know because of it is that, if loss happens – even the worst loss I can think of – I know I can get through it. It'll be sad, it'll hurt, but I'll

The feeling of
aloneness I've
felt exists because
I had oneness
with her.

The feeling of
aloneness I've
felt exists because
I had oneness
with her.

come out the other side into a new-new normal. And I want you to know the same thing. If you can pick your way through all that sadness, you will be OK. Maybe more than OK – you might even flourish.

Of course, in life, nothing comes for free, and often, if there are benefits to be found in getting comfortable with your loss, there's an emotional payoff somewhere. For me – for lots of us – that will be guilt. Guilt that you get to enjoy life, guilt that you've managed to turn your loss into something helpful, guilt that you might even benefit from that horrible situation. But you have to give yourself a break. Nobody's designed to feel bad forever, and if you're beginning to see yourself flourish not in spite of, but *because* of the loss you went through, that's a testament to the work you've done to get there. It's not about pimping out your loss for personal gain – it's about understanding the impact it's had on you, and being honest with yourself about what you need. Once you start looking at that, it's pretty hard to stop. That honesty, once you have it, is a superpower you'll probably never give up. Because it empowers you to live your very best, most authentic life. And to know that it's OK to do that – to reposition your loss not as a stand-alone, untouchable moment, but as a fully integrated part of you – that's when the magic happens. Becoming this new you doesn't mean you're over it. It doesn't mean you'll never be sad about it again and doesn't mean you might not be whipped around the face with it when you least expect it. You're not leaving behind the memories of your lost one – if anything it means you're taking them with you. The microchip version that's assimilated everything you've learned from them. You're you, but different. Upgraded. You've added a few new filters, and the world just looks a little bit changed through them.

If you're an introvert like me, it's likely that you'll start to see those changes happen on the inside first, and the way you talk to yourself, or relate to the world might start to shift a little. Where an extrovert might know they're getting comfortable with loss because they cry less frequently on their friends, we introverts might know it because we're able to cry more frequently with friends – to get our loss out in public to talk about and examine.

Be Adam Sandler

You'll have seen Robyn and I talking about the mental health side of loss in terms of building a little emotional house – every time you do something good for yourself you get another brick to put in it. But no emotional house is stable without solid foundations. So it might be that you need to knock down a few supporting walls and examine a rising damp problem before you can mix your cement, and that's OK. Sometimes two steps backwards is exactly where you need to be. Imagine how shaken you feel by that initial loss earthquake, then imagine yourself moving through the world, safe in your unshakable emotional house of rubber bricks. The house that you built yourself, and that you can have friends over to whenever you like. Doesn't that feel warm and safe? Loss might feel like it's exploded your existing house, but that means you get to rebuild it however you want it, with a new annexe and a pool. Maybe you choose a whole new career sewing quilts, or join a bereavement group and go trekking at the weekends, or take a year off, or adopt a dog or take up karate or enter that competition in the UK where you chase a round cheese down a big hill – life's full of encounters and opportunities you might not have taken without first living through the discomfort of loss. Think of it like the plot of every Adam Sandler movie, ever: you're trundling along, then something bad happens, then you go through a series of difficult and farcical events, before finally emerging victorious, changed, but still Adam Sandler. Just Adam Sandler who's a more comprehensive golfer/ hairdresser/wedding singer. And if that's not the perfect ending point for a note on finding yourself after loss, I don't know what is.

ACTION STATIONS

Exploring your new beginnings when the unthinkable has happened.

- Find five minutes and sit yourself down somewhere quiet by yourself. Try to think of one positive thing that's come out of your loss. If you can't yet, that's totally fine – you have all the time in the world.

- Take a moment and try to recognize any pastimes, relationships or things from your pre-loss life that aren't giving you as much joy as they once did. Be honest with yourself – try not to judge what comes up. Just notice the feeling and sit with it for a little while.

- Grab a pen and write down three pie-in-the-sky, no-holds-barred things you love the idea of doing. It might be to star in a movie, or go to Barbados or build a robot or cure cancer – no limits, what would they be? Pocket that list and add to it any time you think of a new one.

Dr Sheetal Says...

It feels strange to say that you might gain from loss but you really can, as it encourages a reconnection with the world and your place in it as well as way to cope with further losses or life events. You learn about yourself, others and society, and it's a piece of learning (no matter how gut wrenching the loss was for you) that will probably be life-altering.

Take time to look at the person you want to be, your values, and the route you want to take going forward. Introspect on any changes you want to make that you think will improve the way you live your life and tackle any loss anxiety. You went through that loss so yes you'll be able to get through this too. You might gain a sense of confidence and a belief in who you are, or find a sense of injustice that you want to reframe and channel for good. Think about how you made it out of that journey. And what amazing things you've gathered on the way to prop yourself up during challenging times. You're amazing. Please remember that. It does not mean you are glad that the loss happened; it is making the best out of a difficult situation. You don't deserve to feel bad forever.

Now let's get to the practicality of this. It will be hard: the avoidance and anxiety will potentially skyrocket initially, but then it will get better. Think of being on a rollercoaster which could last a few minutes, hours, days or even months, but will end. Build a new narrative around the loss, not at the heart of it. At the heart of it is you. Without change, things stay the same. When conducting trauma therapy, the aim is that the emotional content becomes more distant and less fearful when we come across a trigger. Change is always uncomfortable, like getting undressed in front of a partner for the first time. If you keep not doing it, it'll become a bigger deal and then unimaginable and impossible to bear. Take your clothes off sooner. See how it goes when you get to your undies. So far OK, no one got hurt? Take the rest off. Well done, you've officially achieved growth.

Blood is thicker than water

I'm estranged from my family.

It's a hard thing to say, and
to come to terms with.

But, there it is – that's the
truth of it.

I'm estranged from my family.

It's strange even writing it down.

It's not what I imagined for myself.
Not how I saw my story going.
Not at all.

That first bond, that familial love, isn't always a good fit, however much we wish it was. And when it's not, we can take time to mourn the loss of the future we had imagined, and then – when we're ready – we can start again. On our own terms.

I am estranged from my family. But that doesn't mean I don't have a family – in fact, I have the best family I ever could have asked for. The family I've chosen, and built, consciously and actively. Not *despite* blood being thicker than water, but *because* of that.

"The blood of the covenant is thicker than the water of the womb."

That's the real phrase, the real meaning, and those relationships we choose for ourselves; those are the real bonds that are being celebrated. Chosen Families aren't a consolation prize. Chosen Families are made up of real, deep, lifelong bonds of love that we build, shape, and nurture – and they're just as strong, if not stronger, than those we're born into. Or, at least, they *can* be.

We can choose our own families. Host our own celebrations. Start our own traditions. We can rebuild from the ground up, deliberately, and carefully, and we can fill our lives with new loves, and brand new families, that can last a lifetime.

Author, activist and founder of
@officialmillennialblack, Sophie Williams
on the wonders of chosen families

I GOT YOU, DAVE

So, you know somebody who's lost something? How do you even start to think about being helpful beyond saying, "My condolences," over and over?

Emma: My optimal support thing would be a card containing a really thoughtful, personal message, ideally accompanying flowers.

Robyn: Oh YES.

Emma: Something that says, "I see you, I care about you and I love you, but I also respect your need to process." Until I knew you it would never have occurred to me that what people might want in that moment is to be around other people.

Robyn: I am so grateful they sat there and listened to me just be a bit mad.

Emma: Yeah, that must've felt nice, like you were being wrapped in a big person blanket.

Robyn: It made me feel less entirely desolate. Just loved. Wrapped in love.

EMMA ON HELPING OUT DAVE
How to do good support whether you are or are looking after an introvert

I think it's mine and Robyn's differences that have brought us so close together. Having somebody who absolutely does not get it, but who is willing to stick around, listen and cherish you anyway has been a powerful binding agent. Hurtyness is hard to spot in people who do it differently to you, and as an introvert who needs buckets of time and space, it can feel challenging to understand how being around people and noise can be helpful to somebody else. But, if I'm listening to Robyn, ever, I know it can be just that.

It's a balancing act, this looking-after lark, and what works for one person is going to make another want to hide in a barn. Even if you've been through a loss yourself, and think you have looking after sad people nailed, you probably don't. I know I've got it wrong, especially with Robyn, but also with people built more like me. You might throw yourself into the act of caring, feeling like you know exactly what they need, only to find that, actually, that's what *you* need. And in times of crisis the desire to be of service can blinker signals they're giving out about what would actually benefit them. If this sounds terribly complex and difficult, it's because it is. But fear not, there are ways to be there for anybody, even if you're the staunchest, most hermetic introvert (me) caring for life-long extrovert Robyn. If you're willing to put in a little time, there's much comfort there to be offered, and – as Robyn and I have found – much learning to be had about one another.

Care when you are the introvert
Introverts tend – and this is a generalization – to be quite emotionally intuitive. Because we live such a rich emotional

WHAT DO YOU DO WHEN SOMEONE IS SAD
WHAT DO YOU DO WHEN SOMEONE IS SAD
WHAT DO YOU DO WHEN SOMEONE IS SAD
WHAT DO YOU DO WHEN SOMEONE IS SAD

WHAT DO YOU DO WHEN SOMEONE IS SAD
WHAT DO YOU DO WHEN SOMEONE IS SAD

WHAT DO YOU DO WHEN SOMEONE IS SAD

WHAT DO YOU DO WHEN SOMEONE IS SAD

WHAT DO YOU DO WHEN SOMEONE IS SAD

WHAT DO YOU DO WHEN SOMEONE IS SAD

WHAT DO YOU DO WHEN SOMEONE IS SAD

WHAT DO YOU DO WHEN SOMEONE IS SAD

WHAT DO YOU DO WHEN SOMEONE IS SAD

WHAT DO YOU DO WHEN SOMEONE IS SAD

WHAT DO YOU DO WHEN SOMEONE IS SAD

life inside and don't emote so much outside, we can be quite good at telling when somebody else is hurting, especially if they're doing the quiet sort of hurting we recognize. But when it doesn't look like quiet inside-sadness we might not spot it. When it looks like shouting or partying or constant shopping and distraction, to an introvert, that can be so difficult to read as grief. And indeed, when you're caring for people very different from yourself, the first indication that they're hurting might be a behaviour that rubs you up the wrong way. I, for example, shut down and get uncommunicative when I'm sad, which ends up with Robyn feeling rejected and shut out. Whereas Robyn's more likely to get angry, to which I respond by... shutting down and getting uncommunicative. It took me a really long time to understand that those moments of anger are so often less to do with rage and more to do with feeling vulnerable and needing support. So sometimes it's about looking beyond what the person is saying or doing and asking yourself what could be driving that action. If your introvert instinct is to run away, perhaps that's the opposite of what your person's trying to ask for. It's a bit like learning a new language. For example: what do you do when somebody's sad? My first thought is always to send them a lovely message or a distant gift in the post, because that's what makes me feel loved and nurtured, by people who are – crucially – far away. But I could spend a million pounds on flowers for Robyn and she'd still prefer me to pop over and watch *9 to 5* with her. And I can do that, sometimes. And sometimes I can't. Both are OK. When you're an introvert caring for somebody else, it's more important than ever to keep time and space for yourself, because no good care was ever powered by an empty battery. It might be tempting to rush in with meals and blankets and hugs and tea and company, or to move in and sit with them, talking long into the night, but there's only so long an introvert can keep that up without burning out. So if you're having to be somebody's support network and you're of the introvert persuasion, you're going to want to set some boundaries. Set a mental out of office; rope in other friends and family. It's important to be there for loved ones through a loss, but never at the risk of running yourself down. And similarly, if you are somebody who's been through a loss yourself and you're looking after a loved one who's also lost, be prepared for that to bring up some difficult stuff about your own situation, and try to give yourself time to deal with that too.

I'm gonna take this opportunity to say: oh man, I have got care wrong with friends SO MANY TIMES. I've gone overboard on love and freaked them out, I've waited until the end of a party at 2am to bring up the subject, I've missed anniversaries, I've mentioned anniversaries when the person didn't want them mentioned, I've tried to solve losses, I've been too forceful with suggestions of therapy, and I've projected my own situation onto other people more times than I can remember. Every loss is new and every loss is unique, so it's about working out ways to ascertain what your loss-ee needs, then doing that. It's about understanding that you're coming at it from your own place and set of experiences, and trying not to bring those to the table. And it's about being there, no matter what, for longer than you think.

If you're not the kind of person who's able to be physically there all the time, show your care in other ways. You might want to add key dates like anniversaries or birthdays into your diary so you know exactly when to get in touch, especially if your brain is a master avoider like mine. And if you do send messages, try to keep them feeling normal – the way you'd talk to your friend if they weren't going through loss. Sometimes I think we're so frozen in the face of loss that we forget how to be normal people – we feel like there has to be a degree of reverence and formality about everything, when what the loss-ee needs most is a loving dose of humanity. For example, instead of, "I'm sorry for your loss", which feels like something a robot might say, try something in real-speak, like, "I'm so bloody sorry you're going through this." Instead of, "You must be feeling awful," try, "How're you feeling?" and instead of, "Let me know if there's anything I can do," try, "I'm here if you need somebody to just listen." They're subtle differences, but they make a message feel less like a duty and more like an act of care.

Caring for an introvert when you find introverts hard to read

In the same way that an introvert might struggle to recognize grief in an extrovert, if you're an extrovert, you might not know how to see when an introvert is struggling, because it's happening on the inside. It can be hard for introverts to do their feelings on the outside. Not just hard – sometimes a physical impossibility. Even now, after much therapy, when I have to have conversations with people about difficult emotional stuff my body starts to shake. So those conversations are exhausting. If you're an extrovert caring for an introvert, try to understand how hard it might be for that person to behave in ways you recognize. Because if, to you, loss looks like crying and talking, to see somebody not doing that might make you think they're kind of OK. But their crying and talking is probably happening when nobody's around. When they feel safe to get it all out for a bit of a romp. It might be that they just need space to do emotions. It might be that they need to work out how they feel about everything before they can let you in.

Or it could even be that you seem like a bit of a dangerous person to be around. In the nicest way possible, if you've gone through a loss yourself, or are somebody who's really comfortable talking about loss, being around you might remind them of their own discomfort, or they might be on guard around you in case of questions and probing. I know I did this and I know other people have done it with me – it's OK. And if your loss-ee is a person who seems like they want to be left alone, you can still find ways to let them know you're there – keeping that channel of connection and thought open means that they know there's a place to fall if they need to. If you're dealing with somebody like me, that's not going to be a bi-weekly phone call or afternoon tea, it might just be a hand-written card once a month, or a text message saying, "Just so you know, I love you a lot." Low-key moments that let a person know that they're seen and thought of, and have a buddy if they need one.

If somebody had asked me outright what I needed when my Mum died, I would have – and did – tell them I was fine, to make them feel better. I did that knowingly and willingly. But, honestly, at the same time, I was hurt by people's readiness to believe that I was OK. Complicated, right? In hindsight, what I impossibly wanted was for people to silently read my mind and love me from afar, with low-impact gestures that enveloped me, but left me in peace to process. If that rings true about somebody you know, it's about finding gentle ways to let them know that you care, but that don't require anything in return – to me, that's a beautiful thing. So, if you're looking after an introvert, send flowers if you can. Send a journal. Send a teddy. Send anything that that person can look at when they're by themselves and know that they're loved. Because it's not always feasible or sensible to be there with them all the time. When my step-mum's mum died, I bought her a pair of nice champagne saucers and three mini bottles of champagne for toasting, one bottle to be opened after a week, one after the funeral and one on the year anniversary. But it doesn't have to be fancy – it could be a silly drawing, it could be a big home-made poster that says, "ONE MASSIVE HUG", it could be a cardboard cut-out of George Michael that you know will make them laugh – whatever it is, it's a little touchpoint to let them know that even though they're in a shitpit and you're not there in person, you have them in your heart. And know that the person might not respond. You might never get a word of thanks, or an indication that they got the gesture and it helped. That's OK. They're in Loss Town, and we all remember what a desolate place that can be.

It's so, so hard to see somebody we love hurting. We want to help, and be effective and feel like there's a conclusion, instead of open-ended sad. But sometimes people don't need advice and they don't need a quick fix. They don't need for you to make them feel better. I think one of the greatest emotional injustices we do to people is assuming that sadness needs to be remedied. That crying needs to be cheered away. That feeling bad is a problem that requires a solution. Most of the time, when somebody's sad, they just need to be listened to very carefully, and nodded at, and hugged. Sometimes all you need is for somebody to say, "I see you, I know you're hurting and it's shit, and I'm sorry." There's a time and a place for Doing Things and Getting On With Life, but, chances are, if an introvert is showing you their hurty, squashy inside emotions, it's because they really need you to understand and empathize – you're being brought into the fold, and it's a scary thing for somebody who lives all that stuff by themselves most of the time. So, be gentle, be attentive, ask questions that let them lead the conversation where they need it to go. And resist the urge to try and find a solution – even if you know that your aunt's friend's mum found Pilates when her husband walked out, maybe keep that one in the back pocket for another time.

Team Loss

Of course, everybody feels differently about different kinds of loss. So one person's reaction to losing their pet dog might seem wildly out of proportion to somebody who lost a child. But every loss is embedded in that person's life, experiences and emotional plantation. They don't exist on a sliding scale of importance, and what affects one person in one way will affect another person completely differently, so it's about having compassion, and trying not to judge from your own set of experiences. I think lots of people who've lived through a loss – particularly a loss that isn't a death – have felt the tides of support turn as, six months down the line, friends start to think it's time they got over their divorce/house fire/lost cat. It can be so isolating, which is why support is so crucial, whatever it looks like for you. Robyn and I found our community in each other – two total opposites – and used that weird little dynamic to try and make loss a little easier. That's how this book came about. Through the learning and understanding that what works for one person's loss might send somebody else running for cover. We learned how to have uncomfortable conversations and test the waters and understand when to shut up. This book is my testament to being open and honest about even the worst bits, and I take strength from that. Whatever you go through, and whoever you go through it with, I hope that this will help you to find comfort in each other, to wait and listen with openness and love. Because loss can be truly awful, but sometimes that's when our best people shine.

ACTION STATIONS

How to help an introvert amigo going through a loss.

- Rather than asking to physically see them, keep in touch with a message a day.

- Prepare for them to flake on any in-person plans you might have had. Resolve to not get mad about it. For the rest of time.

- Ask questions like, "How are your feelings?" that allow them to give as much or as little back as they like, without feeling cornered.

ROBYN ON HELPING OUT DAVE

How to support your friends when you are a
noisy extrovert hell-bent on rifling through their
emotional knapsacks

I lay in bed this morning and thought of all the Daves I knew
and how I'd offer them support in a time of loss. It went a
little something like this.

Dave Newman: *A chap who resolutely exercises his feelings into
submission/soaks them away in endless, emotionally cleansing, bath
breaks* = Lots of asking if he's OK knowing I would get no
reply/a humorous one to deflect.

Dave Ward: *A man with the exact same dimensions as a spectacled
bear and all the snuggliness too* = Crawl onto his knee and hug
him for a week.

Dangerous Dave Sephton: *My uncle and a man who, I'm
pretty sure, gave himself that nickname* = Make a brew and strap
in to talk about the thing he lost for four to five hours. The
subject matter will range, be prepared.

Dave Watts: *My father-in-law. Incredibly charming, possibly a
spy. Think Nigel Havers* = Hand squeeze, "It'll be OK, old
chap", and then probably avoid talking about it ever again.
It's in the handsome mahogany box alongside a litany of
national intelligence, like who kidnapped Shergar and the
location of Lord Lucan. He could even *be* Lord Lucan...

And that was actually very helpful because it showed me,
and you, that some Daves are really easy. And well, some
are introverts...

The extroverts. The ones like me. I knew they'd want to
talk and share and feel like someone else got what they were
going through and be bolstered by that. I live for those

Daves. But the other Daves. The quiet, insular Daves who do not want you rooting through their emotional stuff. Well, I find them immensely challenging. Because on paper they don't want your support. When in fact they actually do but they want it in a very controlled way, a way that they aren't obliged to immediately react to, or react to at all. They're already at maximum capacity because experiencing all the emotions at once is quite unfamiliar to them and I can imagine is a bit like that time I did bad mushrooms in Thailand. Everything has gone wibbly. So, they take a more nuanced approach.

I'll come back to the old introverts in a jiffy but probably best to start with me, for that is the natural way of things on Planet *It's Your Loss*. When I am in any kind of funk I want one thing: attention. I want support and I do not want it to be subtle. I want to do a lot of talking things through, I'll embark on a lot of reassurance seeking and invite a lot of hugging. I was very lucky that I have gathered a plucky group of emotional empaths around me who offered me just that when my Nan died and do so in any time of upheaval. My friends still call each other. We're those weirdos. We can be found in cafés (when not in a time of a global pandemic) talking at length about some relationship, dilemma or situation. The majority of them hauled ass to Lancashire when I was in bereavement city, eager for an audience with sad Robyn. I was both distracted by them and given an outlet for the plentiful emotions I wanted to hand to someone else. There were lots of long walks and bike rides and it got me through. One person, my best friend from university, who I think I can say without pissing her off, would also categorize as feeling a bit "other" just sort-of moved into my grandad's farm for a while. I don't know when she arrived or left. She was just *there*. We made a hash of the funeral drinks, got everyone hammered and she was a little bit of scaffolding holding me up. I don't really think there are words to express how grateful I am that she did that and how extraordinary it was for a woman in her early twenties to offer support in that way. She is miraculous.

Being the first in my peer group to navigate a big loss made me feel like I had a handle on how to help others in the same boat. I'm very grateful for that. Because it feels good to be useful. It's shit being the first person and so alone in your experience but there's a solace in being the one who knows how to offer support. Like with my lovely friend Charles, I'm confident I can drop in a "How you feeling about your dead dad then?" loudly enough to alarm everyone at the next table and he'll laugh proudly, tell me he's bested his therapist and basically fixed himself. People like Charles and I are the most simple people to support. We're dying to talk about the thing. Just pop on the green light and we'll whack out what we want airing. There are intermediary people who you have to put in a little groundwork with, skirt around the issue for a while and sooner or later they'll be like, "Oh my god, this is so crap," and away they go. They'll give little breadcrumbs of heartbreak now and then but they don't hold with the three-ring circus. I'd put my Uncle Bryan in this category. He was incredibly close to my Nan. I might even go so far as to say he was her favourite, despite me being in her phone under that particular moniker[1]. Bryan doesn't go in for long stories and lying on the sofa and public outpouring of emotion. He just says something really sad occasionally and you think "Shit, it was a bit impossible

---

1 Put myself in there as that, she couldn't work out how to change it.

for you." But he carries on, without the mum he loved so much, saying very little and when he does it's guaranteed to be a zinger. Then there's the advanced losers. Approach them like a member of the bomb disposal squad but make one wrong move and they won't go off, they'll just pop you on the dangerous list and shut down completely. They do not want pushing, at all. AT. ALL. They are doing DIY devastation and any attempt at intervention feels like an affront. Imagine [insert regally dignified person here] lost someone very dear. And you sent around, say, Donald Trump to rifle through her feelings? Not right. Too loud. Too direct. Absolutely unwelcome. Well that's a very extreme version of the point I'm making.

Now even knowing all this, attempting to offer support can seem absolutely terrifying. People automatically want to offer solutions, and as I've drummed home harder than Phil Collins, loss is a problem there's no solving. So you're left to flounder about trying to say the right thing while freaking out that you might be somehow offensive. Take it from me, there is very, very little you can do to offend someone who's grieving. Apart from just ignoring them. Or saying "everything happens for a reason", or suggesting something like they're just on to the next cycle of their existence.[2] Whatever you say, they'll at best think "Oh that made me feel better, thank you" and at worst be like, "I can't even register that right now", and it'll float away. Or if they're in the extreme category we mentioned, put you on the naughty list. It's not permanent, don't fret. The thing about offering support is that actually, it's not about you, as hard as that is for me to type. The person who is in a mess is not

---

2 DAD. I'm talking to you.

going to be a very good friend, there's no space for that. They won't look at anything with any nuance. There is an above average chance you'll say/do the wrong thing. That's fine. Don't be struck dumb by the fear you'll make a hash of it. They'll only ever remember the silence. That's what stings. Leave your ego at the door and accept that for a while, and I mean a WHILE. This person is going to be a bit volatile and you're going to have to just muddle a way through and you'll do a lot of re-reading WhatsApps to check you didn't do it wrong and maybe they'll seldom reply. The most valuable sign off when texting this kind of person is: "No need to write back, I know it's a lot at the moment." People like Emma make themselves responsible for everyone's feelings so even the most wonderful message adds to their hideous to-do list. "Must be grateful to x, y, z." Give them a breather. Know this is one-sided. That's fine for the next couple of months or years. Someone who's sad about loss is always going to be sadder than you think is reasonable because it's just a long old process. But there are some methods that can be rolled out for anyone and you should experience some success.

Do something just nice

When someone close to me lost anything of note, I used to go flowers. Hard. Always. Flowers say, "I love you, look at these, no response needed." You can't receive flowers and be like, get them out of my house.[3] Flowers are easy. You include a heartfelt message of course to say "I care" but the flowers provide the pizzaz. But as losses became more

---

3 Unless you are a member of my family and you have the weird superstition about red tulips, in which case the flowers, and you, will be out the door before you can say, "Guys, they're only flowers."

frequent and more serious, people who I wouldn't want to give flowers to kept finding themselves in Loss Town. And I realized, maybe it's good to just do a five-minute think and transcend flowers. You can congratulate yourself even more for getting it so right, being spectacularly thoughtful and your person will probably like it better. Just take a while to ponder. There are things that take minimal effort but say "You're in the shit right now, have this, *Je t'adore.*" Maybe it's a week of meal kits. Maybe it's getting a lovely, personalized hanky ('cos that is next-level). Maybe it's a soft thing to hold or a nice thing to smell. Maybe it's something all about the thing they lost or nothing at all. Maybe it's a bottle of prosecco and an invite to come drink it on a balmy afternoon if the loss isn't a biggie. Or maybe prosecco even if it is a huge loss because your personal Dave would find that kind of blow-out helpful. It could be poetry if they'd actually like it. Just something that for a moment makes some element of their life easier or better. As I've said before no amount of money can solve this, not even a walking talking dead dad hologram ★coughs, Kanye★ or buying the entire business that sacked them and reinstating them as CEO or having their dog stuffed or whatever. This is not a solutions driven exercise, it's about providing a very brief moment of comfort.

Diarize

That is the most not-Robyn thing I have ever typed. I miss meetings all the time; I think Trello is the devil. I know roughly five birthdays off by heart and a lot of those are directly in relation to my own birthday. But your calendar is going to be of such use to you in times of loss because it will remind you that you have forgotten the abject misery your pal is in and to check on them. Short-cut to looking super supportive right there and knowing they will be very grateful someone is thinking of them even if they don't have the energy to tell you so. I'm telling you so. You can put in a daily/weekly/monthly one depending on how often you want to pop up, the nature of the loss and the kind of support you want to offer. If it's something that's going to loom large, whack that yearly reminder in − for the anniversary if applicable or birthdays now missed or big days when everyone stomps around shouting, "Look at my living breathing mum − I LOVE HER" and that friend is in a ball under the bed. Or times that not being part of the club feels very lonely, like big religious holidays where everyone gathers together. Any time you figure things might be hard then be ready to acknowledge that, say you get it and that you're there. Be reminded to check in about healing injuries, family tensions, tinder dating, general glumness, new house woes and everything in-between.

Commit to the long term

For me, the single most irritating thing to experience as a person navigating loss is the palpable desire for you to go back to normal. Because unfortunately, you're changed now forever − be that in a major or a minor way. You can see it written across rictus grins or in slightly exhausted sighs that people just want you to be fun again. Everyone has moved on and you seem like a drag now. It's all relative. People will tell you to get over the fury that your dad actually had a mistress most of your life, warn you that you're talking about your ex too much, stop asking about your really difficult fertility journey or actively avoid you if you're sad about a bereavement or a long-term estrangement or anything that isn't cheery. If you want to be a good pal, know you're basically getting a massive downgrade on the friend you signed up for, for a while. Know that you'll be that same monotonous, melancholy bugger at some point and you'll be so glad all your friends didn't quietly zone you out then either. You will be Fun Bobby off *Friends*, when Fun Bobby stops drinking and then his grandad dies. Not an attractive prospect. Look at this as part of a lifetime though, your friends or relatives or whoever are going to be with you for the long term, you can put up with them being a bit crap for a little bit, can't you? Good, now readjust all your expectations for them 'cos it's unlikely they'll be your disco pal for a bit – unless it's to attend Club Cry-At-Your-Leisure which would be really weird as it's very much a solo, possibly naked pursuit.

Be led by them

It's a suck-it-and-see scenario AND the rules change all the time. That's nice, right? Be led by your person though. If they want to talk, lean into that. If they clam up, don't push them too hard. They'll be changeable in a way they have no control over and that's really tough for them and for you. Just take it a day at a time and be prepared to amend the comms plan frequently. Sometimes they might want to go dancing 'til dawn. Sometimes they'll want deep chats. Sometimes they'll say they want to dance 'til dawn and actually what they wanted is deep chats and you'll end up weeping on a sofa at 4am looking like a Lady Gaga tribute act that got booted off the bill and are drowning their sequin sorrows. All bets are off, so be prepared to be very bloody adaptable. Be direct if you can. If it would help them for you to say "What would make you feel better now?", and then you do that thing, then do it. Remember though, you need to find a balance between support and enabling, if that's an issue. Don't be the go-to all-night-drinking-buddy if that's a nightly occurrence or get them heroin or diet pills or something ridiculous even if they tell you it will fix them because it will not fix them. If you can't be direct, just do your best, watch them closely, see what they seem to respond to or not and be reactive to that. Be persistent. It's very easy to give up when someone is giving you NOTHING. But you can't, I'm afraid. You have to see this thankless task through to the end.[4]

So Gather ye Dave-friends while ye may, Old Time is still a-flying; And this same flower that smiles today, Tomorrow will be dying to bastardize a famous poem. Time is not standing still, this too shall pass[5] and you just have to stick with it. You'll have a version of your Dave back and that Dave will be just the person to turn to when a big loss hits. May that time be a very long time away, when your Dave is the same age as the current David Attenborough.

---

4 Joke's on you – there is no end but one day it'll be your turn to be the party princess so you'll have your time to shine.

5 To quote someone else, again.

ACTION STATIONS
How to do care with extrovert appeal.

- Physically see people. If you can, go to them. It's a lot easier to be honest and vulnerable when someone is in your front room.

- Be the friend you wish you'd had. I had the friend I wished I had, luckily, but if you haven't, go through all the times you've been offered top-notch support and see if any of it would be applicable to your Dave's loss.

- Give them a get out of jail free card. Maybe a little note saying you know things are going to be heavy for a really long time but you, amigo, are going nowhere. Just knowing you don't have to put on an act can be a wonder.

Dr Sheetal Says...

Remember that what you need after suffering from a loss and what someone else needs may be entirely different. It is what makes us human! The best way to approach this is to simply ask someone what they need. They may say to talk or they may say to be alone. You might get it "wrong" (according to the person you're delivering care for) but at the end of the day, that person will likely understand you are trying to be there for them. Don't expect that others will want to be treated in the same way you do, and be wary of some people needing to please others by saying that they're ok whilst trying to avoid being a "burden" or making you and others feel bad or uncomfortable.

Try to gauge whether you need to be there physically or whether gestures from afar might be better at this stage. Recognise the hurt they are going through plus any other pressures on them, related or not. Perhaps social pressures are too tough to follow through with, so don't give them a hard time if they can't or don't want to do certain things. Make sure they know that you don't need them to be the "normal" them right now, and you're happy with whoever they need to be until time and processing helps to settle things. Don't ask for anything in return. Be flexible – they are probably just as uncertain about their journey as you are. But keep popping in to check.

Solutions to your friend's sadness don't belong in the initial throes of the loss. If you spring practical advice on them prematurely it could make them feel unheard or as though they have no reason to be upset. Ask yourself if this is your own anxiety of sitting with someone else's sadness making you feel uncomfortable. Are you projecting your own need to make it all better onto your friend?

Finally, when looking after someone else and trying to be there for them, make sure you look after yourself too. You won't be any use if you are not fully switched on.

Joe: But hey, how are you doing, man? How are you feeling? What's the weather like in your head?

Adam: Errr, do you want glib answer or real answer?

Joe: Real answer? Or whichever you feel most comfortable in giving me?

Adam: Right, not that good.

Joe: Oh.

Adam: I have to be honest and actually it seems to have coincided with the real weather taking a bit of a downturn but no, I mean the thing is my mum died, very unexpectedly.

Joe: *supportive hmm*

Adam: And I was totally sideswiped by it. [...]

Joe: I am so, so sorry. That's so sad. She was a very elegant and lovely woman so that's awful.

Adam: Thanks man. And as usual thanks for your sympathy and as usual thanks for your. Oh, I'm gonna... *sniffs*

Joe: And it's particularly, as your dad's funeral was such a lovely event. With so many of us getting together, right? And it was such a memorable and good time so it's a great shame that can't happen again.

Adam: It will. It will. I was going to say that one of the nicest letters I got was from your mum. *gulps*

Joe: Why does my mum write to you? She wrote you something when your dad died that was very important, right, and I don't know what she wrote. Don't tell me. But it's very intriguing, she's got some sort of magic.

Adam: Yeah it's a kind of kind, formal directness. She just pitches it exactly right. Not too mushy, not too profound, not too bossy. It's just what you want to hear.

Adam Buxton chatting to long-time friend and film director Joe Cornish on The Adam Buxton Podcast

MIC DROP

Pick it back up again – it's your karaoke party now.

Emma: We've graduated from Loss University with a Bachelor's in being alright, sort-of.

Robyn: I guess that proves that the system works.

Emma: That if you can spend time with your loss you'll get more comfortable with it?

Robyn: Yeah, you'll feel less like you want to fold in on yourself, and one day, probably when you've been doing something wildly disconnected from it, you'll be like, "Yes, now I feel better."

Emma: I think that's the crux of it all – you start feeling better when you're least expecting it. You might give it a whole bunch of focus and work on it, and then all of a sudden when you're not looking you realize you don't hurt so much anymore.

Robyn: You really do. And not by poking at it and willing yourself to feel better.

Emma: The hard bit, I guess, is that the end of this book isn't the end of the loss journey.

Robyn: Oh no, it's a stop on the journey, but at least you can enjoy this stop 'cos you're not crying, and can be a bit more optimistic about the rest of the trip.

Emma: The book is the monorail you take to get to the starting line. The monorail runs on tears.

Robyn: Oh, what happens at the starting line?

Emma: You run a very long, slow marathon. And sometimes go the wrong way, and sometimes people overtake you, and sometimes you follow the wrong group of runners for a bit.

Robyn: Oh god yes.

Emma: What's your main hope for the person reading this book?

Robyn: That they feel a little less alone in it all. You?

Emma: That they know they don't have to feel bad forever.

Robyn: I hope we did that.

Emma: Me too.

ROBYN ON HER MIC DROP

Final words from the let-it-all-hang-out, support-seeking extrovert who learned the value of taking a step back in order to help others. Which handily also included herself

So that's that then. Problem solved. Except it isn't at all. But hopefully you feel like someone's given you some serviceable directions to the hardware store where you can grab some of the tools to start whittling away at the problem. It's a big block of ice and you want to chip at it until you have a tiny but resplendent luge. We both know that is going to take ages. But, you get a luge. So...

I'll stop using humour as a defence mechanism now. The issue with loss is that it's both a passive and an active thing to go through. Some of the feelings, emotions and occurrences will just happen. And that's tough, particularly if you're like me and need control over everything at all times. You can't make yourself not feel an absolute mess – even with all the therapy we've tried to foist on you. But you can get comfortable with the notion that:

a. that mess you are in can be useful;
b. you can look at the mess and not be blinded by it like you would looking straight into the sun, and;
c. one day you'll feel it less acutely 'cos you'll have untangled it and it'll be just piles of stuff.

At the start, you have to remember that someone has removed a bit of you[1]. You'll be so achy. It will take time for

---

1   Because really, for you, the lost thing only exists in the way it existed for you, to you. All very *Matrix*, right? There is a completely unique loss-shaped hole and it's scissored out of a non-life-threatening bit of you.

all the sinews to begin to knit back together and for a while the slightest knock will be unbearably painful and fuck some of that healing up. But it IS healing. You ARE learning to live with this. It WILL NOT kill you.

The thing I realized, 11 years on from losing my Nan and four years on from consciously misplacing my Mum, is that those first few years are desperate and freewheeling and come in hideous high definition with surround sound. Everything feels so ever-present and even if you're working through your situation, you're working through it like you're an athlete training for the Olympics. It's everywhere. It's everything. It may involve a terrible diet or compulsive exercise or feeling like you're jumping through lots of hoops. You don't get a medal in the end but you do get to stop running towards it.

It makes me really tired to think about the energy I needed when I was first bereaved. The focus it took. The scale of it. To look at it now and be able to not have to immediately take an action is wonderful. You will get there. It feels like my loss and I have been together for a lifetime, and like any relationship some of the urgency is gone, as is some of the excitement and a bit of the romance. I don't rush home to sit with my grief, cradle it and examine it until I've committed every centimetre to memory. Instead it has morphed into something more predictable, quiet, though still part of my everyday. I love that. I love the loss I have now, compared to the one then. It is so knowable. It's mainly compliant. It has shaped me in some pretty OK ways. I would prefer my Nan back, no question. But the new me and the relationship I have with myself, my experiences and my Nan are ongoing and pretty good. I feel like I understand me/her/it better and though she's not around, I am still adored and guided by who she is and who not having her made me. I dig that.

Emma and I have marvelled, continuously, about how much this book has taught us. How we've been able to articulate, or even just get to a point of consciously acknowledging things about our past that were massive but not as massive as a dead mum. We've been able to work towards getting comfortable with the loss of those things as well. We have given shape to concepts that felt too precious or too terrible to touch. And we've seen how we could use the shitty situations we respectively found ourselves in to help. Primarily each other, and HOW, but also you. It was like re-watching *Jurassic Park* and seeing that yes, it was still an incredible spectacle but also noticing the little inconsistencies. The illusion is broken and the T-Rex becomes just latex and metal and gubbins and it can't eat you and it's just a film. A very excellent film but one you can now turn off in the middle to make a cup of tea or that won't keep you up all night because it's just a load of clever camera angles and good acting. Life's like that – just a load of stuff that if you can't step back and see as all its respective components can seem really bloody insurmountable.

But that's a lot of what this book has been for us. I want to say what I hope it is for you. I want it to be a companion. The opening line of a conversation. A creative writing prompt. A little voice saying, "It's going to be OK, somehow."[2] We want you to feel that by breaking things down into bite-sized chunks they're easier to digest, and by not delivering them in a hushed voice with a gentle nod and an arm squeeze that actually, they aren't too awful to talk about. To laugh at. Because laugh away, you're having quite

---

2 I'll say that in the audiobook and then you can just play it over and over.

the shocker my friend and some of it might be terribly funny, or funny because it's so absolutely terrible. We hope it helps you feel OK about acknowledging the small losses and the profound effect they can have too. To feel like just because your friend has a dead mum doesn't mean you can't talk about your own discomfort at losing your uncle, or the sadness you experienced when your step-mum left, or how after uni you felt really bleak because a wonderful time had just come to an end and now you didn't know what the fuck was going on or ANYTHING. It is all a sliding scale. I have said that too much but I believe it too much. We want you to feel like you can look at those things and not worry you're self-indulgent because they affected you and they need airing. We want you to feel you have two people who get that and that are on your side. We want you to feel that you have a few handy tips that might help you start navigating your loss. We can't give you the answers but we can help you start asking the right questions. We want to initiate a dialogue and then you carry it on. You see where it lands for YOU. We want to be a comfort when we mainly only had each other for that. We want you to feel, even for a tiny moment, a smidge better and that maybe, in the fullness of time, there's a way through this.

We just want to be helpful. We really hope we are.

EMMA ON HER MIC DROP

Final words from the under-sharing, people-pleasing introvert, who discovered the power of sharing and pleasing her dang self

So, how do you feel? Better? Worse? Sad? Hopeful? Overwhelmed? Angry? Horny? Like you might want a sandwich...? All valid responses to reading a book about loss, especially if you read the book to help with your own loss. I think both of us have gone through all of those emotions and more while we've been writing it. Me? I'm sitting here writing the outro to the book I wrote about my Mum dying, so I'm probably cured, right? Well, unless you mean cured in the meat form, and I've been preserved by my own salty tears, no. You can never cure loss – it's always there, because you never get the thing back. Even if you do get the thing back, the loss still exists because it's still something you went through. But your loss gets less sharp. The pointy end rounds and it becomes more of a companion than a murderous threat. A pleasant café instead of a jail. And that café is where I'm sitting, looking at my loss. Mostly comfortably, sometimes sadly, but usually able to get it out and turn it over in my mind when I need to. Loss, my Mum and everything else attached to it, used to be a looming thing – like a heavy bag I could never put down. Now I've had a look through it, put the bits I need in my pockets and left the bag behind, so I can carry on through life, hands-free. Which is great for being able to get other stuff done and find out what else you're about. Having done the brave bit and given myself and my loss enough focus to process what happened, I find myself in the very strange position of being not in crisis for the first time I can ever remember. The constant worry, the peaking anxiety, the guilt and self-loathing –

they're no longer my go-tos. They might pop up from time to time, but in more of a distant fashion. My brain may want to ramp up for a real meltdown, but usually it just doesn't have the gumption. It's a strange feeling. Freeing. A bit confusing, because, really, I've no idea what comes next. But it feels powerful; solid. My little emotional house has its foundations and they were dug by a good builder, laid with love by a worker who cared. I miss my Mum – man alive, do I miss my Mum – but it's a clean, healthy sort of a miss instead of the messy terror I could never bring myself to look at. And she's here. She's here with me because I bring her with me – all the good bits and all the bad bits – that rich sort of a person-dom that she was.

I ummed a bit about using the word "brave" back there, because it can sound a bit grand. We tend to think of bravery as big acts of heroism – rushing into battle when you're likely to get skewered, or jumping into traffic to rescue a kitten – but bravery comes in many forms. If you're prone to stuffing everything in an emotional lockbox, it's those small, everyday acts of bravery that will do you the biggest service through a loss. The moment you allow yourself to sit with what happened, the times you stay still and shed a tear instead of rushing to get on with things; they might feel small, and you might not feel very brave while you're doing them, but motion towards something that scares you – that, my friend, is brave in the extreme. And at the core of everything we want for you in this book is just that. Great courage, doled out in small portions. We often want to move away from loss; we want to get over it, feel better about it. Loss is hard to look at. And when that looking feels like sitting in a bath of nails, it takes a whole bushel of strength and grit to do it. It'll be uncomfortable and you might have some nails wedged in some places for a while, but with time and self-love and kindness, you will find your comfort, get out of the nail bath and carry on knowing yourself a little bit better.

It takes a long time to get used to something or somebody you loved just not being there anymore. But that's loss. It's shocking, sad, lonely and something we all go through. For a lot of us it won't be linear, and for a lot of us the work we have to do will be unexpected and hard. Maybe at times it will feel insurmountable, but mount it you will. With a bit of self-gallantry, you'll find your way through. Sometimes you won't want to. Sometimes you'll curse the world that gave you this much pain – heck, you might even want to stop the ride and get off. But, if you take one thing from our book, make it this: loss is not the end. This thing that might feel like the worst thing; this un-look-at-able monster in the closet – with the right support and dedication you will find ways to sit with it. You'll be able to feel it and continue the relationship with the thing you lost. It's possible. And if this book is for anything, it's to help you get yourself to that place. So whatever you lost, however you're feeling right now, let's just stop. Close your eyes. Take a breath and tell yourself: this is not the end. You are worthy of the time and effort it takes to feel better. It's possible to find peace in all this. Your relationship with your lost thing is not over. Because we're all stronger and more resilient than we think we are. Whatever you use this book for – learning, meditation, kindling – know that it comes with a comforting hand on the shoulder from us, and the sort of knowing, respectful nod heroes give each other at the end of action movies. Because, if you're getting to grips with loss, to us, you are the best damn hero of them all.

if you're getting to grips with loss you are the **best damn hero** of them all

HELP IS OUT THERE

If you need support, there's something out there for you. From free therapy to books and back, use this list to start building your own little emotional house

FOR HELP WITH MENTAL HEALTH

You can access therapy whatever you're struggling with and whatever your personal circumstances but some routes are longer and more unwieldy than others. Here are some suggestions from us – we hope they set you on the right path:

You can find a charity through the NHS who will support you and MIND has an exhaustive list of ways you can gain access to therapy on the How to Find a Therapist section of their website.

Who your counsellor is is crucial and seeing yourself reflected back is something many take for granted – people of colour can look to organizations like BAATN (the Black, African and Asian Therapy Network) and Black Minds Matter for free mental health support and counselling.

If you are in the position to pay for therapy, have a look through the directory of practitioners on the BACP website. Here, you can scroll through by location, by your needs or by the sort of therapy you want. Make a list of a few who sound good and try to arrange a call with them.

If you feel bad, speak to somebody

The main thing to know is that if you're feeling bad, you're not alone. There are people and support networks out there who can and want to help. And if things feel really bad and you're experiencing suicidal thoughts, call the Samaritans or

CALM and talk, just talk. It doesn't matter what you say – just get somebody who's listening on the phone and let them steer the ship for a while. You're always worth it.

FOR HELP WITH BEREAVEMENT

There are as many ways to lose someone as there are people to lose and there is an organization designed to help you work through your own particular bereavement. Head to ataloss.org for an idea of the kind of organizations there are out there. The Good Grief trust even have a map of services in your area – mega useful.

If you find sharing helps, you could try meetups through organizations like Talk About Loss, there's one for you whoever you are and wherever you find yourself in your grief journey.

Or maybe you like to listen and learn, in which case podcasts like Bereavement Room and Grief Cast might be for you.

If you prefer the emotional aid to come to you, you could try signing up to the newsletter of one/all of the amazing members of the grief community doing great outreach: Alicia Forneret does a corker.

For help with the loss of a child The Miscarriage Association have loads of resources listed on their website or head to tommys.org for dedicated support after child loss.

And for specific help when you're bereaved through a suicide, try Suicide & Co, CALM or the SOBS helpline and website for support.

FOR HELP WITH ESTRANGEMENT

Check out charity Stand Alone who do lots of incredible work with estranged adults. With resources, blog posts and a podcast, they're here to raise awareness and support you. There is also a great support group on Facebook called Necessary Family Estrangement run by the wonderful Sali Hughes – drop on by if you want to feel less alone.

FOR HELP THROUGH LOSS OF MOBILITY OR HEALTH

Scope.org.uk are dedicated to equality for disabled people, and have loads of information on their website, including how to find and give emotional support. There are also sites like supportline.org.uk and belize.com that can point you in the direction of applicable organizations who should be able to help. If you've experienced a change in health or mobility, always feel empowered to ask your healthcare providers where you could access support for your mental as well as your physical health.

FOR HELP THROUGH A SEPARATION

You'll find lots of great resources and support through relate.org.uk and youngminds.org.uk have some great information on supporting a child through your separation.

If you're a single-parent family, gingerbread.org.uk are there to support, with resources and stories which can be so useful when you feel you're going it alone.

FOR HELP WITH INFERTILITY CHALLENGES

Head to fertilitynetworkuk.org for a whole host of support from people who get it and supportline.co.uk have a list of support resources on their website for anybody who's living with infertility challenges.

Comedian Rhod Gilbert set up HIMfertility to offer information, support and a safe space for men to learn more and open up their own conversations.

There's a private Facebook group called Men's Fertility Support, dedicated to men's fertility and you'll find a lot of great information for men and women on Fertility Network UK's website.

FOR HELP WHEN YOU LOSE YOUR CAREER

For the practical bits, head to nationalcareers.service.gov.uk to find out what steps you can take to keep your finances going and get the support you need.

Possibilitychange.com is a website dedicated to talking about big life changes, and has some great support for anybody grieving a career.

FOR HELP AS A NEW PARENT

There's loads of helpful stuff on the nct.org.uk website, about being a new parent and about dealing with post-natal depression, whether you're a Mum or a Dad. As we've said, there are also so many amazing parents just laying it all out online so do head to social to find some amazing parent support networks.

FURTHER HELPFUL READING FROM OUR CONTRIBUTORS

- Adam Buxton, *Ramble Book: Musings on Childhood, Friendship, Family and 80s Pop Culture*, Harper Collins 2021
- Kayo Chingonyi, *A Blood Condition*, Chatto & Windus 2021
- Catherine Cho, *Inferno: A Memoir of Motherhood and Madness*, Bloomsbury 2020
- Alicia Stubbersfield, *The Yellow Table*, Pindrop Press 2013
- Kae Tempest, *Running Upon the Wires*, Picador 2018
- Sophie Williams, *Millennial Black*, Harper Collins 2021

OTHER'S DAY

A way to help the parentally-challenged feel less sad and alone

If you don't have a parent around or you can't be a parent yourself, you'll know how uncomfortable reminders of that fact can be. Little moments that pop around and tickle your psychological tonsils until you want to vom emotions over everything. Most of those moments you get to deal with in private, by taking yourself off and doing a spot of self-care, but when it's Mother's Day or Father's Day, it can feel like the whole world has collaborated to show you just how very alone you are. The card shops filled with cards, the marketing emails, the supermarket displays, the social media posts, the ad campaigns, the chats on WhatsApp – a million micro moments that hold a magnifying glass over whatever pain you have about your own situation.

The two of us had always found those days and the run-up to them difficult. They're wonderful ways to celebrate great parents, but in being that, they just left us in a high state of missing our best ones. Then one day we realized if we were feeling like that, maybe other people were too, and we started to talk about it a little on our Instagram accounts. About how those times of year could leave people anxious and sad, or angry and vulnerable. We could never have predicted the response we got. Hundreds of people dropping into our DMs to tell us their stories – it was an overwhelming outpouring of grief and relief and love, and it showed us how much people had been hurting inside, each believing they were the only ones. So we set up our #othersday campaign online, which gives anybody for whom parent days are challenging a space to come and share over Mother's and Father's Day, when those wounds can feel at their most raw.

You'll find us on @othersday or on our blog All Up In My Space, sharing and caring for all we're worth. We've been honoured to be let in on people's stories of estrangement, of miscarriage, of bereavement, of growing up in care, and over the years it's shown us how much of a need there is in the world for frank, honest conversations about loss. To speak openly about the realities of traumatic experiences, without fear of judgement, without worrying you're not doing it right, and without it needing to be *terribly serious* all the time. Because, in our experiences, you don't stop being funny, weird, wonderful you, just because you went through loss.

That's how Other's Day was born. We share blog posts, coping mechanisms, stories and ideas; conversations with those who've lost, ways to help yourself get through the day. It's an incredible movement powered by our community and shows us each year how much love there is in the world.

INDEX

ACKNOWLEDGEMENTS

Firstly, to all the women who made this book happen, we're enormously grateful. To Cathryn and Jess for believing it could be a publishable book and fighting to make that happen. To Steph, Bess and everyone at DK for being so behind it – together we created something really brilliant. To Amy, our editor, who has been the cool, calm and collected cat we needed every step of the way, and a master footnote pruner – thank you for your patience, all of it. To Sheetal for making sure we aren't being medically negligent and basing our ramblings in some kind of psychological fact. To our contributors – some old friends, some new – for sharing the most intimate parts of your lives in the hope that you can make other people living through similarly hard times feel a little less terribly alone. You are AWESOME. To the people who spoke about this stuff before us and the ones who'll come after, and to everybody who's ever joined in with Other's Day, for being the brave souls who made us think this book might actually be a help. You make our little hearts sing.

Emma would like to give some acknowledgements...

To my Robyn, my D-Bag, my totally opposite buddy who I learned so much about while writing this book. You've taken me on a journey from the bowling alley, through an inflatable assault course to these pages. Every step of the way has been weird and new, and I thank you for coaxing me onto it. We've been through so much together, and story-told our way through the rest, so that I actually now feel like we're related. The loss-based version of the movie *Twins* (you can be Danny DeVito). Thank you for working so hard to understand my way of being. Thank you for charging forth when I need to hang back. For being big when I need to be small. For being my fearless, brightly-coloured, shaven-headed amigo. You changed my life forever, and that is a wonderful madness.

To my Dad, who cried when he picked me up from the station and who I'm proud to be building a new kind of relationship with. To Lesley, my step-mum, and Jackie, her sister, for being the friends my Mum needed in her darkest hour. To John and Noreen, who put a tiny courgette in a man's Diet Coke and to Elizabeth for showing my Mum that people really liked her. To my friends who stuck with me when I didn't want to see anybody, who gently prodded me out into new situations and who folded me up into their groups like I always belonged. To Matt, for always trying to understand, and just wrapping me up a big hug when you didn't. For not leaving, even when I've pushed you away, and for being a solid, unflappable, vulnerable, silly and ever-evolving presence in my life, that I'm learning I can rely on. You are my favourite person.

And lastly, but never leastly, to my Mum. The place I belonged most in the world was in one of your hugs and there's a you-shaped hole in my heart forever. This book's for you - the one you never got to write, and I love you so very much.

Robyn would like to give some acknowledgements...

I've done a lot of acknowledgements along the way, in the form of meandering personal anecdotes so I'll attempt to keep this short.

To everyone who's ever mothered me, which turns out is a heart-warming number of people. To teachers: especially Mr Mills, Mrs Custard and Mrs Nicholson who were so gentle and nurturing when I was on a knife-edge – weird to go back but you caught me at a tipping point. And Mummy Bear, of course. To the classmates who made me believe I could write and pushed me forward with their own, much better, writing. James, Mike, Paul and Christof, you are excellent.

To the families that absorbed me. To my excellent friends, too numerous to list and who I'm not going to attempt to in case I forget someone. To the ones that became family. To Rachel who has made me feel normal in being not normal since we were perma-tanned teens. To Aurelie, who swooped in and held all the pieces of me together when I couldn't – I wish I could have done the same for you. To the colleagues who became friends, professional mentors and encouraged me to carry on in a world we all knew was bedlam: Sophie Kirk, Ed, Madeline, Mike, Andrew, Jenny, David and LAURA. Wonderful Laura who listened to me moan about this process pretty much every day for a year. I owe you a gin and pineapple. To Ally for giving me a second chance at Christmas. To Jess for the three-hour nightly phone calls and being my long-distance support system.

To my family. Who can be so infuriating but are also all the books I want to write. I feel so privileged to be a part of our potted history and though our stories don't always have a happy ending, you are where I have been happiest. To some people who went above and beyond: Uncle Bryan, Auntie Sue, Auntie Hilary – thank you for seeing I needed something when I couldn't see it myself.

To my courageous, complex, wonderful Dad – thank you so much for staying. And for giving us a home that we could trust in. I adore you. And my brother, the only person who really gets any of it the way I do. To my other brother: I miss you. And to my Mum – I hope you find the contentment that has always eluded you. To Buddy – the cab of your tractor was my sanctuary and there aren't enough drunken phone calls in the world to adequately express how grateful I am.

And to the people who aren't around anymore but were so central to who I am now, especially Nan. It's all for you, Lovely Barbara. I wish you were here to be proud of it, because even if it's an abomination I know no one would be prouder. And to see you with the cover printed on a sweatshirt/baseball hat/superimposed on the side of the car would have been wonderful. And mortifying.

To my husband who is the single greatest person I ever met and has showed me that life can be quiet and predictable and full of the kind of love that you don't have to scream into each other's faces. I am astonished that you chose me every single day. Thank you for allowing me to avoid packing up the third consecutive house move to finish this book. I wonder what the next excuse will be. Thank you to your family for being my touchpoint for sanity, always.

And to Emma, someone who started off simply looking like my (much hotter) sister and ended up being one in every sense of the word. I wish you could see how incredible you are. Considering you're my partner in words, it's embarrassing how hard I find it to jot down the levels of gratitude I feel at the fact I have someone so uniquely good and patient and strong and clever and funny and inspiring to take this pretty shitty journey with. I couldn't have done it without you. You are my best friend. I could not be me without you. Never leave. JOKES[1].

1 Also, a bit not jokes